Designing
Interpretive Signs

Principles in Practice

Designing
Interpretive Signs

Principles in Practice

Gianna Moscardo, Roy Ballantyne, and Karen Hughes

Sam H. Ham, Editor
Applied Communication Series

Fulcrum Publishing
Golden, Colorado

Library of Congress Cataloging-in-Publication Data
Moscardo, Gianna.
    Designing interpretive signs : principles in practice / Gianna Moscardo, Roy
Ballantyne, and Karen Hughes.
        p. cm. -- (Applied communication series)
    Includes bibliographical references and index.
    ISBN-13: 978-1-55591-550-6 (pbk. : alk. paper) 1. Signs and signboards.
2. Visual learning. 3. Visitors centers--Educational aspects. 4. Exhibitions--Educational
aspects. 5. Museums--Educational aspects. 6. Historic sites--Educational aspects.
7. Parks--Designs and plans--Educational aspects. I. Ballantyne, Roy. II. Hughes,
Karen, 1964- III. Title.
    HF5841.M67 2007
    302.23--dc22

                                                                2007021435

Printed in Canada by Friesens Corporation
0 9 8 7 6 5 4 3 2 1

Cover and interior design: Patty Maher
Cover photographs (clockwise from top): National Museum of Australia,
Canberra, Australian Capital Territory; Kronosaurus Corner, Richmond,
Queensland; Eden Project, Cornwall, United Kingdom;
Mount Field National Park, Tasmania.

Fulcrum Publishing
4690 Table Mountain Drive, Suite 100
Golden, Colorado 80403
800-992-2908 • 303-277-1623
www.fulcrumbooks.com

Contents

Chapter Seven

Chapter Eight

Chapter Nine

Chapter Ten

Foreword

Sign, sign, everywhere a sign
Blocking out the scenery, breaking my mind ...
—"Signs," Five Man Electrical Band, 1970

When the Canadian rock group Five Man Electrical Band wrote these lyrics, they unwittingly captured one of the most perplexing problems in the interpretation profession: the proliferation of signs. And there is some truth behind their objections. Ill-conceived, poorly designed, and inappropriately placed signs continue to clutter the landscape in some of the world's most special places. Moreover, signs are often the site manager's first choice among communication media because they're relatively inexpensive to produce and have the potential to communicate important information over a wide geographic area where paid staff simply can't be. So when a new interpretive need pops up, it's easy to erect "yet another" sign.

However, as valid as these concerns are, they point not so much to the number of signs in a given place as to the quality and communication effectiveness of the signs that are erected. Indeed, signs are essential in most interpretive settings, and studies show that they remain an appealing information source for visitors. Without signs, many interpretive programs simply could not achieve their missions. Recognizing this, Gianna Moscardo, Roy Ballantyne, and Karen Hughes have joined forces to author *Designing Interpretive Signs*, one of the most comprehensive and readable volumes ever produced on the use of signage in interpretation.

What appealed to me most in inviting this book into Fulcrum's Applied

Communication Series was the combined experience of the three authors and their deep understanding of the interpretive signage literature. Virtually every conclusion they draw and the recommendations they offer about the design, content, placement, and evaluation of interpretive signs are based on the findings of current research. Much is known today about why some signs succeed when others fail, and the authors have masterfully assembled that body of knowledge in what I believe is an unprecedented attempt to give practicing interpreters the best available and most comprehensive advice on interpretive signage anywhere in the world.

Readers of these pages will find themselves immersed not only in the artwork of sign production, but in a delightful presentation of the strategy behind the art. Drawing on advances in cognitive science, Gianna, Roy, and Karen carefully walk their readers through the entire process of conceptualizing a sign based on its purpose and aims and proceeding through proven methods for attracting attention, provoking thought with strong themes and targeted content, considering issues related to sign location and placement, and gaining evaluative feedback both before a sign is produced and after it is installed. Most impressive about this volume is that it puts the audience at the center of the decision-making process in a way that few other books on this topic have done. In communication, all things are audience-dependent, and the authors' thoughtful consideration of audiences' tastes, preferences, and tendencies underpins the advice offered in every chapter. In particular, chapter eight (Designing Family Exhibits and Signs) stands out as a long-overdue addition to the interpretation literature. Since most interpretive settings cater to the needs of family groups with children, the ideas presented in this chapter about reaching children with signs that are also intended for adults will stimulate many readers to think differently about interpretive signage in public areas.

Designing Interpretive Signs is destined to become one of those volumes that interpreters everywhere will want in their personal libraries. Rarely have I had the joy of editing such a meticulously prepared yet easy-to-read manuscript. Who knows? If the Five Man Electrical Band could have read these pages before they composed their hit song "Signs," they might have written different lyrics.

Sam H. Ham, Ph.D.
Professor and Director
Center for International Training
and Outreach
Department of Conservation Social Sciences
University of Idaho, U.S.A.

Deputy Director
Tourism Research Unit
Monash University, Australia

Preface

An important feature of interpretive signs and exhibits is that they are designed for multiple audiences. In the same way, this book has been designed to appeal to interpreters, both experienced and new; students of interpretation; and researchers seeking to explore and understand interpretation and its outcomes. Our overall goal is to provide people working and researching in this field with a summary of research evidence and current knowledge about how visitors respond to the many messages and media used in interpretive settings.

One of the challenges for those seeking to communicate about interpretation is to ensure that they practice what they preach. To this end, wherever possible we have incorporated features that match interpretive design principles, such as

- catchy titles and a little humor to "lighten the load";
- summaries of the key points for those who are in a hurry;
- chapters and sections that stand alone so readers can select the information that is of most relevance and interest to them and/or read the book in the order that best suits them; and
- examples and illustrations to make the principles and research "come to life."

We have used signs from many different types of visitor settings to illustrate our points. It is important for the reader to understand that there is no such thing as a "perfect" sign. In the words of one of the author's supervisors, "There is no such thing as a weakness there are only emerging strengths." All the signs in this book have both "actual strengths" and "emerging strengths," and we encourage the reader to focus on the "actual strengths" noted in the captions.

All new knowledge grows from existing knowledge, and all books rely heavily on the advice of colleagues and editors. The authors wish to acknowledge both the dedication of the researchers whose work is used in this book and the extensive efforts of the series editor, Professor Sam Ham. Sam's comments and suggestions have encouraged us to continue this endeavor and to improve our performance in too many ways to mention.

Chapter 1

Setting the Scene:
What Are Interpretive Signs and Exhibits?

Signs—Here, There, and Everywhere!

Signs are an integral part of modern leisure experiences. They tell us where to park, where we can walk, how to behave, and where to look; they tell us about the environment, wildlife, and views and vistas. Signs give us an insight into the lives, loves, and hardships of people who lived in the past, people from other cultures, and people who live in countries and places very different from our own. Signs can pique our curiosity, challenge our perceptions of the world, expand our knowledge, and bore us to tears. Signs tell us things that fascinate, excite, revolt, and amuse us. Signs can be so witty and cleverly written that they make us laugh out loud. Others are so confusing and badly written that they make us yawn with boredom and frown with frustration.

Visitor centers, heritage sites, museums, art galleries, and tourist attractions all rely heavily on signs and exhibits to convey information and ideas to visitors. In many instances, these take on the role of "tour guide," informing visitors about the features, events, and objects they encounter. Well-written signs can make the experience "come alive" for visitors, and provide them with meaningful, engaging experiences. However, unlike tour guides, signs do not allow the audience to ask questions or clarify content, cannot answer visitors' questions face-to-face, and cannot be regularly altered to suit individual needs. Consequently, signs must

be particularly well designed if they are to interpret environments, objects, and events in a manner that is meaningful for visitors.

The range of signs seems endless, but what makes a sign "good"? How do we design signs and exhibits that attract, interest, teach, challenge, and inspire visitors? How do we ensure that the passion we feel for a topic is conveyed to visitors? How can we use signs to motivate visitors to think and care about the features, environments, objects, and events being described? Finding answers to these questions is important because visitors are becoming more widely traveled, more knowledgeable, more sophisticated, more experienced, and as a result, more demanding. Simply throwing together a sign that contains a smidgin of historical information with a map and some old photographs is no longer acceptable, and in today's competitive tourism environment, it is unlikely to guarantee your attraction's long-term viability! Thus, the aim of this book is to explore what makes a sign "good" and discuss ways in which interpreters and educators can research, design, produce, and evaluate their signs.

Before delving into the features of effective signs and exhibits, it is useful to consider the function of different types of signs. Signs are generally divided into three categories, depending on their function: orientation/information signs, warning signs, and interpretive signs.

Orientation and Information Signs

Many visitors approach interpretive sites, museums, and visitors' attractions with little idea of where to go or what to do. Finding their way around can be quite intimidating, so providing orientation signs that clearly outline what visitors will encounter is invaluable for putting them at ease. Essentially, orientation signs are navigational tools that help visitors pinpoint their current location and find their way around. They depict the location of facilities, such as drinking fountains, picnic tables, cafeterias, and restrooms, and often include maps and/or plans of the whole area to give visitors a bird's-eye view of the site or attraction. Orientation signs are also useful for helping people plan their visit—it's very common to find visitors sitting at the entrance to large exhibits poring over a map and getting themselves organized. Be aware, though, that some people have difficulty translating two-dimensional maps into three-dimensional features. If your site is complex, consider drawing landmarks in relief to enable visitors to easily match the feature with what they see (Falk and Dierking 1992).

Signs or maps that list opening times, visitor facilities, activities, and attractions are generally referred to as information signs. They provide the basic information required to plan a visit to tourist attractions and heritage sites, and may be located at visitor centers, on roadsides, or at the attraction itself. Sometimes information signs situated at the attraction incorporate features that have an orientation function.

Regardless of their content, orientation and information signs are usually located at the entrance to a site or attraction. They may include directions on how to get to a specific section or exhibit and are often repeated regularly throughout the site, particularly at the beginning of each section or themed area. Some visitor settings also use colors to code different display areas for ease of navigation. For example, the National Gallery in London has divided its collection of 2,000 paintings according to when they were painted. Paintings are displayed in four separate areas, each color coded and clearly delineated on orientation maps as well as at the entrance to each area (Hooper-Greenhill 1994).

Visitors generally won't read introductions for long, as they are eager to start exploring (Serrell 1996a). For this reason, the best orientation and information signs have short sentences and limited information. They should also be written in a format that can be read at a glance—the last thing you want is a crowd blocking your entrance because they are trying to read your sign! Good orientation and information signs are written in layperson terms that provide a clear indication of what each section/exhibit/feature entails—it makes little sense to use labels such as "Creatures of the Mesozoic" if most visitors do not realize this means dinosaurs (Hooper-Greenhill 1994).

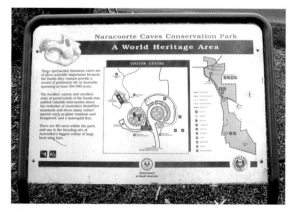

Figure 1.1. Signs can help you plan your visit.

Warning and Safety Signs

Warning and safety signs inform visitors about potential dangers associated with their visit and provide messages about how they can enhance their personal safety. Effective warning signs clearly identify the threat as well as specify the human behavior associated with, or contributing to, that threat (Ham and Krumpe 1996). As an example, signs that aim to persuade people not to feed wildlife should identify specific aspects of the practice that are problematic (such as wildlife attacking humans for scraps) and highlight the human behavior that contributes to or perpetuates the problem (hand-feeding wildlife in picnic areas). Warning and safety signs are usually located where the threat or danger is likely to occur (Ballantyne and Hughes 2006).

Figure 1.2. Signs can try to keep you safe.

Interpretive Signs

Interpretive signs provide information about a place, object, or event that enhances visitors' appreciation, understanding, and enjoyment. These signs translate facts, figures, and concepts into a format that attracts, interests, educates, and inspires visitors. Interpretive signs rely heavily on the use of stories and messages to give visitors insight into key elements of the topic being

discussed. Essentially, interpretive signs take on the role of tour guide or teacher, enabling you to talk to visitors when you can't actually be with them.

Interpretive signs or labels can be found

- In zoos, wildlife parks, aquariums, and botanic gardens
- At museums and art galleries
- In historical houses and heritage sites
- In national parks, local parks, and forests
- As single signs associated with a particular object, place, or event
- Along a trail or walking path
- As part of exhibits in visitor centers

As we will discuss shortly, to be considered interpretive, signs and exhibits must adhere to six basic principles of interpretation.

Interpretive Signs and Exhibits—Why Bother?

There are two very good reasons to have interpretive signs and exhibits in tourist attractions and heritage places. First, interpretive signs and exhibits can enhance the quality of visitor experiences. Because satisfied visitors are likely to return and recommend an attraction, interpretation can improve the financial viability of many tourist and heritage places. Second, interpretation can help in the management of visitor behavior by explaining how visitors should behave and encouraging them to care for the places they visit.

Laying the Foundations: Interpretive Building Blocks

The key ingredient in quality interpretation is the ability to excite, delight, and awaken the senses; in essence, interpretation connects to the core of the human spirit—our beliefs, experiences, hopes, and dreams. The aim of interpretation is to translate ideas and concepts into a format that captures, engages, entertains, and inspires audiences. In the same way, interpretive signs translate the principles and practices commonly associated with effective visitor interpretation into a written and often illustrated format. Although interpretive signs and exhibits may contain facts and figures, they go beyond focusing on the "oldest," "longest," and "rarest" by explaining the significance of an object, place, or event in a way that enriches visitors' understanding and experiences. Effective interpretation "leave[s] people moved, their assumptions challenged and their interest in learning stimulated" (McArthur 1998, 63). Table 1.1 presents some formal definitions of interpretation—note the common features they share, such as the emphasis placed on enhancing visitor understanding.

Interpretive signs and exhibits can be used to inform visitors about places, buildings, historic figures, flora, fauna, natural environments, ecosystems, objects, artifacts, cultural practices and beliefs, towns, industries, activities (e.g., spear making, organic farming), historical periods, and events. You can use them to give visitors a sense of place; to instill new ideas; to excite, inspire, and teach; to conserve natural and cultural resources; to reinforce or refute existing beliefs; to enrich recreational experiences; and to enhance people's understanding of their relationship to their environment and culture (Ballantyne 1995; Carter 1997; Knudson, Cable, and Beck 1995). Essentially, interpretive signs and exhibits explain something to your visitors in a way that entices and interests them, but also clarifies the subject matter. As an example, most people are familiar with scissors and how to use them. But how many of us know what a Tibetan prayer wheel is or how it is used? To be fully understood and appreciated, a prayer wheel needs to be explained or interpreted (Carter 1997).

Regardless of the topic, there are six basic principles for effective interpretation that apply to all types of interpretive tools. Interpretation should

1. Make a personal connection with, or be relevant to, the intended audience
2. Provide or encourage novel and varied experiences
3. Be organized with clear, easy-to-follow structures
4. Be based on a theme

Table 1.1 Some Formal Definitions of Interpretation

Interpretation is the process of explaining to people the significance of the place or object they have come to see, so that they enjoy their visit more, understand their heritage and environment better, and develop a more caring attitude towards conservation.
—*Society for the Interpretation of Britain's Heritage 1992*

Interpretation is a means of communicating ideas and feelings which help people to understand more about themselves and their environment.
—*Interpretation Australia 2004*

Interpretation is an educational activity which aims to reveal meanings and relationships through the use of original objects, by first hand experience, and by illustrative media, rather than simply to communicate factual information.
—*Tilden 1977*

Interpretation is a planned effort to create for the visitor an understanding of the history and significance of events, people, and objects with which the site is associated.
—*Alderson and Low 1985*

Table 1.2 A Summary of Three Sets of Interpretive Principles

Tilden (1977)

➤ Any interpretation that does not somehow relate what is being displayed or described to something within the personality or experience of the visitor will be sterile.

➤ Information, as such, is not interpretation. Interpretation is revelation based upon information.

➤ Interpretation is an art, which combines many arts, whether the materials presented are scientific, historical or architectural.

➤ The chief aim of interpretation is not instruction, but provocation.

➤ Interpretation should aim to present a whole rather than a part and must address itself to the whole man rather than any phase.

➤ Interpretation addressed to children should not be a dilution of the presentation to adults, but should follow a fundamentally different approach.

Ham (1992)

➤ Interpretation is entertaining.

➤ Interpretation is relevant.

➤ Interpretation is organized.

➤ Interpretation is thematic.

Moscardo (1999)

➤ Make personal connections to visitors and get them involved.

➤ Create clear content and tell a good story that makes sense.

➤ Provide variety and encourage participation.

➤ Know and respect audiences.

➤ Allow for alternative audiences.

5. Engage visitors in the learning experience and encourage them to take control of their own learning

6. Demonstrate an understanding of, and respect for, the audience

These principles form the foundation of all effective interpretation and can be used as a template when designing any form of interpretive activity, whether it is a guided walk, an interpretive talk, a workshop, or an interpretive sign. The six principles are based on Tilden's (1977) principles for effective interpretation, Ham's (1992) EROT principles, and Moscardo's (1999) mindfulness principles. These are summarized in Table 1.2—note that there are several related and recurring ideas that appear in each set of principles (e.g., the notion of placing emphasis on personal connections, using themes, and provoking or entertaining visitors).

In the remainder of this chapter we will discuss the six core interpretive principles and provide suggestions about how they can be used to design signs and exhibits that interest, inspire, and inform your visitors.

Principle One: Interpretation Must Make a Personal Connection with, or Be Relevant to, the Intended Audience

Research consistently shows that people assimilate new information by relating it to something they already know (Ballantyne, Crabtree, Ham, Hughes, and Weiler 2000; Moscardo 1999). Well-designed interpretive signs and exhibits have clear, simple explanations that bridge the gap between new information and visitors' existing knowledge and experiences. The importance of providing information and experiences that have

Table 1.3 Visitor Comments on Personal Connections and Relevance

The analogies the woman used were ones that any child could understand. It was really great. (32)

You really learn more if there is a story or an experience. You can look all day ... but if it all comes closer to home, you remember more if you can come closer to the objects. (29)

You can handle the objects, touch them and feel them. You're not just looking in, but you can be part of it too. (34)

Source: Wolf et al. (1979).

meaning and personal value for visitors cannot be overstated. Dazzling graphics, interactive activities, and educational content will count for very little if visitors are unable to make meaningful connections with their previous knowledge and experiences (Screven 1999). In the words of visitors themselves, "It's something personal that you can do. A lot of these buildings are so big it makes you feel lost. When you get a chance to have a personal thing like this you don't feel so lost" (Wolf, Munley, and Tymitz 1979, 30).

It is also clear from comments made by visitors that finding or making a personal link with the interpretive material is a major factor influencing their satisfaction and learning. An analysis by Wolf et al. (1979) of visitor responses to exhibits in a Smithsonian museum provides support for this conclusion. (See Table 1.3.)

Such comments suggest several mechanisms for providing personal connections. These include the use of humor, analogies, and metaphors to build links between the interpretive content and visitors' everyday experiences; telling stories, particularly those

with characters that visitors can relate to; and providing visitors with opportunities to interact, participate, and make choices about their interpretive experiences. Visitors generally like being challenged and appreciate being given suggestions about how to apply their newly acquired knowledge in their everyday lives. They also appreciate the opportunity to ask questions. Although this is not generally possible if interpretation relies on signage alone, this requirement can be accommodated to an extent by ensuring that your signs and exhibits answer questions commonly asked by visitors: What is this? What is it used for? Who uses it? and Why is it here? Techniques for incorporating these features into your interpretation are discussed further in chapter five—a brief example to illustrate our point is presented in Table 1.4.

Even if the exhibit deals with topics beyond the experience of most visitors, interpretive signs can be made relevant by

Figure 1.3. Making personal connections with the reader

Table 1.4 Using Personal Connections to Interpret the Topic of Fruit Bats

Humor	How does something so small make so much noise?!
Analogy	Bats sleep all day and party all night—just like teenagers!
Metaphor	Bats: hundreds of black umbrellas hanging on a tree
Stories	Basil the fruit bat wakes up every day just as the sun goes down. He yawns, stretches, and lets out a loud screech ...
Interaction	Step through this door to experience the sounds and smells of a fruit bat colony!
Application of new knowledge	If you don't want to share your garden with fruit bats, think very carefully about the trees you're planting!
Questions	How does a bat hang upside down without getting disoriented?

focusing on aspects that relate to the "here and now." For example, a display describing the history of an area could highlight the similarities between modern life and life at the turn of the nineteenth century:

The platform where you are standing now once overlooked a verdant rain forest that stretched as far as the coast. This lookout has been popular since the beginning of the last century, when Victorian families used to travel here by horse and buggy to admire the view and have a picnic, much the same as families do today.

Likewise, unfamiliar objects can be interpreted by highlighting their similarities to common ones. For example:

Ficus opposita: *Aborigines rub the leaves of this tree on skin infections such as ringworm prior to treating them with bush medicine. This plant is often referred to as the sandpaper fig, and if you feel its leaves you'll know why!*

Visitors may not recall the scientific name for this tree, but by linking the leaves to an everyday object (sandpaper), they will probably remember its uses and common name.

Principle Two: Interpretation Should Provide or Encourage Novel and Varied Experiences

Humans as a species instinctively pay attention to differences and changes in their environment. This also applies in visitor settings—people tend to mentally "switch off" in environments that have repetitive signs, exhibits, displays, or information. This is problematic because if visitors are not paying attention, it is virtually impossible to communicate with them.

So how can we ensure that our settings are varied enough to maintain visitors' interest and attention? A common approach is to design exhibits and signs that incorporate different media, such as audiovisual presentations, models, computers, music, and interactive displays. You can also introduce variety by supplementing exhibits with entertaining activities and games, such as quizzes, treasure hunts, and craft workshops. To capture and maintain visitors' attention, these should incorporate an element of fun, and should be presented and perceived as entertaining. This doesn't mean that the interpretation should be trivial or superficial, but you ought to keep in mind that visitors are in leisure settings, not classrooms (Carter 1997). Indeed, according to Ham (1992), entertainment in interpretive settings can take on many guises, but the key underlying characteristic is that interpretation does *not* resemble traditional classroom instruction. This is a call to exercise creativity. Design signs and exhibits that are quirky, engaging, and entertaining—ones that your visitors will *want* to look at rather than ones they feel they *should* look at. The added advantage is that if visitors are engaged and enjoying themselves, their learning and recall are enhanced (Ballantyne et al. 2000).

Introducing variety and novelty encourages visitors to pay attention, but is it possible to maintain visitors' attention and interest the entire time they are in the leisure setting? Research suggests possibly not. Falk, Koran, Dierking, and Dreblow (1985, 255) observed visitors as they moved through a whole museum and concluded that visitors "allocated their attention in a consistent pattern. They spent the first few minutes orienting themselves, the next half-hour intently attending to exhibits, and the remaining 15 to 30 minutes 'cruising' through the balance of the museum, stopping occasionally to look carefully at some of the exhibits." Similar patterns have been observed by other researchers, suggesting that after an initial burst of interest, visitors tend to move through exhibits as though they were browsing. Unless there is something particularly eye-catching or interesting, the chances of them stopping to absorb interpretive messages are slight. Again, it is the interpreter's job to design unusual, quirky, clever, and engaging signs and exhibits that "stop visitors in their tracks."

The positive benefits of a change in pace or style in an interpretive setting or activity are clear in the comments of visitors themselves. An evaluation study by Wolf et al. (1979) at the Smithsonian Institution in Washington, D.C., found positive responses for Discovery Corners, which offered both contact with a guide and the opportunity for interaction with objects. When asked why they rated the experience so positively, visitors often referred to a different experience, novelty, or change of pace from the other activities and exhibits available:

- "It breaks the monotony of pace— which is good."
- "I never saw a presentation anything like this in a museum before. It's a good idea."
- "It wouldn't be good to have these all over the place but here and there it gives you something different to do." (33–34)

Principle Three: Interpretation Should Be Organized with Clear, Easy-to-follow Structures

The content of any interpretation needs to be organized so that visitors can both access and follow it. Interpretation that is based on sequential experiences (such as guided tours, performances, and videos) can be structured into an introduction, body, and conclusion because interpreters control the order in which information is received. With signs and exhibits, however, interpretation is often nonsequential because it is the *visitors* who decide the order in which they access information. Studies in a range of museums and interpretive sites show that visitors are highly selective in what they view. Some visitors read signs and view exhibits in-depth (known as "studiers"), some browse through exhibit areas (known as "strollers" or "browsers"), and some skip from exhibit to exhibit, spending only a few seconds at each one (known as "streakers" or "skaters") (Knudson, Cable, and Beck 2003). The order in which signs and exhibits are viewed is often random, but the one thing all groups have in common is that they usually read the title first (Ham, pers. comm., n.d.). Titles should therefore be eye-catching, interesting, and thought-provoking, but not trite, clichéd, or full of jargon (Dean 1994). A good example is in Australia, in an exhibit in Tasmania's Strahan Visitor Center that discusses environmental pollution along the banks of the King River. Its title "River of Death" immediately draws visitors into reading the accompanying text because they wonder who or what died, and how.

Once you have developed an eye-catching title that clearly states your theme, organize text into a hierarchy using headings and subheadings. Important information and key messages can be presented in a larger font to attract attention. This layered approach helps visitors to learn because it provides them with a mental scaffold for the interpretive content. It also allows visitors to quickly decide which signs or sections of signs to read. We discuss and illustrate techniques for organizing text into layers in more detail in chapter six.

If your site or exhibit area has a structured one-way system for visitor viewing or you have several signs and/or exhibit panels that are viewed in a set order, your first sign should introduce and clearly define interpretive themes and topics contained in the whole set. If you don't do this, your visitors may have difficulty comprehending the subsequent signs and exhibits. For example, Hooper-Greenhill (1994) describes an exhibition on eighteenth-century scientists that failed to successfully convey concepts because many visitors did not have a sufficient enough grasp of this historical period to put the information into context. She suggests that an introductory sign with key events and facts about the eighteenth century would have helped overcome this.

Figure 1.4. A clear introduction

At the end of sequential exhibits it is customary to present a concluding sign that reinforces the messages and concepts discussed, and acts as a "punch line" for the whole sign or exhibit (Ham 1992). Too many interpretive experiences simply peter out, giving the impression that interpreters either ran out of space or inspiration or both. This is a wasted opportunity, as conclusions are your chance to pack a punch, to drive home your central themes, to summarize the exhibit in a powerful way, to encourage reflection, and to emphasize the highlights of a sign/exhibit (Knudson et al. 1995).

Principle Four: Interpretation Should Be Based on a Theme

Themes are the underlying ideas or "take-home" messages about the topic being

Figure 1.5. A take-home message is a good way to finish.

discussed. They provide the foundation on which the whole interpretation is built and enable visitors to comprehend and recall new information (Ham 1992; Pierssene 1999). Effective themes attract visitors' attention; they are specific, stimulate interest, and enable visitors to make important connections between their experiences and the feature being interpreted (Pierssene 1999). Basically, themes provide visitors with the "big picture" by helping them understand and connect the different elements of their visit.

Many themes can be developed from a single topic—it is important to select one that has maximum impact and best conveys the message you intend. As an example, the topic "forest regeneration" could be interpreted using several themes: "New life emerges daily from the forest floor"; "Forests are constantly evolving and changing"; or "Careful logging ensures that forests continue to grow." The choice of theme would depend on the content of your exhibit, the information being communicated, and the core

message you want visitors to absorb and think about (Capelle 1995). The key to developing appropriate themes is to ask, "If *I* were the visitor, what would *I* really want to know about this area/topic/object?" It is important to keep in mind that effective interpretation involves reiterating the theme(s) throughout the visitor attraction. This means that the theme(s) chosen must logically link to all exhibit elements, not simply one item, sign, or exhibit (Dierking and Pollock 1998). These issues will be discussed further in the next chapter when we present guidelines and case studies illustrating how to select and develop appropriate themes.

Principle Five: Interpretation Should Engage Visitors in the Learning Experience and Encourage Them to Take Control of Their Own Learning

Providing opportunities for visitor participation and interaction has many benefits. First, it introduces that all-important ingredient, variety, into signs, displays, and exhibits, which, as we've already discussed, helps to keep visitors focused and interested. Second, it personalizes the experience, making the interpretive material more meaningful for each visitor. Third, it gives visitors a sense of control over the experience because it enables them to do as much or as little as they wish.

The importance of allowing visitors choice in interpretation is demonstrated by a study that examined the differences in visitor responses to computer exhibits with three levels of visitor participation (Moscardo 1999). The first level was a quiz game that required very little participation—visitors could only choose from a series of multiple choice answers that were presented in a set order. The second level was an information program that allowed visitors to choose the topics and levels of information given. The third level was a story game in which visitors could both personalize the story by playing the part of a character and control the program by choosing the topics, actions, order, and locations of the story components. The study revealed that increased choice and opportunity for participation were associated with more positive outcomes, such as more time spent interacting with the exhibit, higher enjoyment ratings, and higher levels of self-reported learning.

Although research examining the benefits of interactive elements is limited, it does appear that visitors enjoy activities requiring some form of participation, and that they are more likely to remember activities with more interactive elements (Caulton 1998; Hooper-Greenhill, 1994). Thus, as interpreters we need to strive to provide interactive experiences in which visitors are able not only to participate, but also to *choose* whether and how much to participate. In other words, when designing interactive experiences you should give visitors some degree of control. This may be as simple as a sign that encour-

ages them to lift flaps to answer questions, or as complex as a multimedia virtual reality experience that allows visitors to create their own museum. The key ingredients are providing visitors with the opportunity to do something that makes the experience more meaningful (smell, taste, feel, lift, or push) and giving them a choice about how much or how little they will participate. Some of the many ways you can incorporate interactive elements into your signs are presented in Figure 1.6. We discuss the design of interactive elements and present examples of some successful interactive exhibits in chapter four.

Principle Six:
Interpretation Should Demonstrate an Understanding of, and Respect for, the Audience

Tilden (1977) was particularly concerned with the need for interpreters to respect visitors. He reports that interpreters often have a "tendency to overestimate the background the tourist brings to the scene and on the other hand to underestimate the intelligence of the 'average visitor'" (Wissler quoted in Tilden 1977, 46). Many interpreters find it difficult to accept that visitors may not share their own interests or background knowledge. The solution lies in recognizing this fact and finding a common ground. Serrell (1996a, 48) proposes that interpreters should see their audience as "a self-selected group of semi-motivated, time-limited, mostly first-time visitors, who are novices but curious about the subject matter ... [who] are seeking gratification through feelings of competence and an enjoyable social experience."

Visitors differ both from each other and from interpreters in many ways. Although it is common practice to distinguish among visitors in terms of demographics such as age, sex, and nationality, research indicates that many other distinctions influence

Figure 1.6. Interpretive signs and exhibits can be about more than just reading.

responses to interpretation. These include previous experience, motivation, activity preferences, membership in social groups, and whether they visit in groups or alone. Differences between international visitors and local residents, for example, are often disguised differences between no experience and substantial experience of a place or topic. These differences can affect the time visitors spend in an interpretive place, the level of interpretation they want or expect, their preexisting knowledge, their existing attitudes, and the content they seek.

What options exist for dealing with different types of visitors? Some of the principles and guidelines we have already described offer some solutions. For example, giving visitors variety in, and control over, interpretive experiences provides opportunities for them to have experiences that are best suited to their different needs and interests. You may also like to think about providing different layers or levels of information for different groups (see chapters seven and eight for more detail). Another obvious option is to have some understanding of the particular audience for an interpretive activity or place. Indeed, knowing about your visitors is clearly of value, not only in terms of planning for alternative audiences, but also for designing content and providing personal connections. If you know how much visitors understand about certain topics and concepts, you can design signs

and exhibits that capture visitors' interest, anticipate and answer their questions, and address common misconceptions (Ballantyne and Packer 1996). We further explain techniques for appealing to a range of visitors in chapters five and six and procedures for exploring visitors' interests, knowledge, and experiences in chapter nine.

Key Points

Interpretive signs can enhance visitors' understanding, enjoyment, and appreciation of the objects, events, and sites they visit. They cover topics ranging from descriptions of fauna, flora, and geological formations to historical accounts, scientific phenomena, and modern technology. Although the range of topics is virtually unlimited, we consider signs as "interpretive" if they have the following key characteristics:

- They make a personal connection with, or are relevant to, the intended audience.
- They provide visitors with novel and varied experiences.
- They are written in clear, organized structures.
- Their content is based on a theme.
- They give visitors choices and encourage them to get involved in the interpretive experience.
- They demonstrate an understanding of, and respect for, the audience.

Chapter 2

Look Before You Leap:
Planning Interpretive Signs and Exhibits

Designing effective interpretive signs requires detailed planning and careful consideration of the messages you want visitors to understand and accept. Before discussing the processes involved in planning and designing an interpretive framework, it is important to state that not every site, feature, or event is suited to interpretation. Indeed, Tilden (1977) claims it is almost impossible to interpret beauty or spectacular scenery, and that in such cases, the place should be allowed to speak for itself. Likewise, quiet reflective contemplation may be the only option for places of reverence or worship. As an example, the only interpretation provided at a World War II concentration camp site in Germany is a wall of photographs taken on the day of liberation. The site itself is completely devoid of life and eerily quiet—the emptiness creates a sense of desolation that speaks louder than any number of interpretive panels ever could. The point is, before rushing in to design your interpretive talks, exhibits, and signs, consider whether interpretation will enhance the visitor experience. If you think it might, read on.

One Step at a Time: The Interpretive Planning Process

There are many models and systems for developing interpretive plans (see Brochu 2003; Ham, Housego, and Weiler 2005; Knudson et al. 1995; and Trapp, Gross, and Zimmerman 1994 for more details on effective interpretive planning). All have three core steps or phases in common:

1. Defining the objectives of the interpretation
2. Turning objectives into themes
3. Selecting the best interpretive medium

Regardless of your site and/or interpretive content, any signs or exhibits you design must support and be guided by an interpretive plan.

Defining Objectives

Getting started is a daunting task when developing any form of interpretation, so it's useful to have a "plan of attack" to ensure that key issues are addressed. Questions you should be asking in the initial design phase include the following.

What Is Special about
This Place, Event, or Object?

Answering this question requires researching the special properties or aspects of the topic(s) you want to interpret. What you're looking for are features that make a place important or unique in some way. These could include animals, plants, and other features of the natural environment, which might include spectacular mountains, waterfalls, escarpments, and views; cultural traditions and celebrations; historic events; human stories; buildings; artifacts; and opportunities to participate in unusual or special activities, such as diving with sharks or watching turtles hatch (Ham et al. 2005). There are several national park manuals that set out detailed procedures for identifying features of natural, cultural, and historical significance and determining the value of each of these for inclusion in an interpretive plan. The following Web site provides an example for the Forestry Service of British Columbia, Canada: www.for.gov.bc.ca/ric/Pubs/Culture/rec/index.htm. Although the procedures are often detailed in several pages, the core principle is to create a list or inventory of features that could be used to tell an interesting story to your visitors.

What Are the Visitor Management Issues?

For many tourist attractions and heritage places, part of the interpretation plan will be focused on how to encourage visitors to behave in a way that minimizes negative impacts both on the site and when they return to their homes. To do this effectively, you need to carefully consider what it is you want visitors to do and how you can encourage and support this behavior. For example, telling visitors to keep off the grass isn't effective if there are no paths or boardwalks as alternatives.

To be successful, interpretation must combine the objectives of both interpreters and management (Ham 2003). Thus, if the objective is to raise awareness of the effect of land clearing on soil salinity, you could design signage around themes such as "Trees give life to future plants" or "Trees keep our soil healthy."

What Are the Constraints of the Setting or Place for the Interpretation?

Addressing this issue involves identifying the resources you have available for interpretation by asking questions that might include the following:

- Are there extreme weather conditions that make interpretation difficult?
- Is there enough space for large groups to hear/see your interpretation?
- Does your site have alternative uses that might interfere with the interpretation?

Factories, construction sites, and crowded areas might be too busy, noisy, and dangerous for interpretive activities.
- Will the interpretation affect other people who aren't visitors? Interpretation in churches, homes, and workplaces might be intrusive for those who live and work there.

Who Is the Audience?

Surprisingly, one of the most common mistakes in interpretive planning is to forget about or ignore the audience. Often interpretive plans focus on what *interpreters* want to say rather than on what visitors might want to hear. The challenge for any form of interpretation is to ensure that the messages presented reflect the interests and concerns of your audience. For example, as an ornithologist you might be fascinated by the breeding cycle of rainbow lorikeets, but is the average visitor likely to share this interest? Probably not. They're more likely to want answers to questions such as "Why are they so brightly colored?" "What do they eat?" "Why are they so noisy?" "How can you tell which is male and which is female?" "How do you teach them to talk?" and so on.

In addition to accommodating your audience's interests, it is useful to consider whether visitors may be constrained by

- the time they have available,
- their safety and comfort needs,
- the group with whom they're visiting, and
- how much they already know about a topic.

A good option here is to conduct some front-end evaluation using surveys, interviews, and/or observation to find out who your visitors are, what they are interested in, and how they currently use or are likely to use a site. Chapter nine describes this type of

Case Study:
Flinders Chase National Park, South Australia

A visitor survey conducted in Flinders Chase National Park, South Australia, included a section designed to develop an understanding of what visitors required from a proposed new visitor interpretive center (Greenwood, Woods, and Moscardo 2000). Two questions focused on potential topics for the new center. One asked visitors to rate their level of interest in sixteen potential topics, and the other asked them what questions they would ask a park ranger.

The five most popular topics were (1) the wildlife visitors might see in the park, (2) interesting geographical features, (3) hints on how to see the wildlife, (4) hints on how they could minimize their impacts on the environment and the wildlife, and (5) the prehistoric animals that once lived in the park. The five least interesting topics were (1) pastoral land use, (2) lighthouses, (3) biodiversity, (4) fire management, and (5) weed management. These findings were consistent with what visitors reported

they would ask a park ranger, namely

- Where do I find the wildlife?
- When will the roads be improved?
- Will there be more guides in the future?
- How is the environment maintained with large visitor numbers?
- Why was Flinders Chase designated a national park?

These questions were used to develop interpretive signs and exhibits in a new visitor center. Figure 2.1 is an example of one of the wildlife viewing signs developed using this visitor information. A postoccupancy evaluation of this center found a significant decrease in visitor questions about how to see wildlife and an increase in visitor satisfaction with their wildlife experiences.

research in more detail, although some examples are provided here to illustrate the importance of understanding your audience before developing the content of your interpretation.

Adams (1993) conducted front-end evaluation before designing an African American exhibit at the Henry Ford Museum and Greenfield Village in Michigan. This indoor-outdoor history museum was planned in part to interpret a house in the village that had belonged to slaves in the 1840s and following years. Interviews with visitors to the museum were conducted to develop an understanding of what visitors would expect from the interpretation of the house and what they already knew about the historical period to be interpreted. The surveys indicated a strong desire on the part of visitors to have African American on-site interpreters. The surveys also indicated that visitors had many false conceptions about the lives of slaves. The

interpreters used this information to develop a self-guided audio tour that addressed these common misconceptions.

Another example that illustrates the value of front-end evaluation is presented in the Flinders Chase National Park case study.

Figure 2.1. Helping wildlife viewers in Flinders Chase National Park, Australia

The last question in the Flinders Chase case study is an important one and, according to several textbooks on interpretation, should be at least part of the major theme of interpretation in any heritage place. According to Knudson et al. (1995), this is referred to as the genius loci and answers the question "Why am I here?" Such information can be used to explain the importance of a site and may act as a "motivator" for visitors to learn more—signage dealing with genius loci issues should always answer the "so what?" question that might be in a visitor's mind.

Turning Your Objectives into Themes

Once you have defined your interpretive objectives, you need to develop themes to achieve these objectives (Ham 2003). But what exactly is a theme? Serrell (1996a) talks about using a single "big idea" to guide the design of interpretation.

In more formal terms, themes have been defined as

- "the message to be conveyed. The theme, in a sentence, provides a concise cognitive overview of the central idea that you will reveal in more detail" (Knudson et al. 1995, 312).
- "always answering the questions 'why is this important?' and 'why should I listen?'" (Knudson et al. 1995, 313).
- "a sentence—a statement—of what the [interpretation] is about. It is a statement in one sentence, with a subject, an action, and a consequence" (Serrell 1996a, 1).
- "the key concept that this particular panel will be designed to interpret. The best way to determine the theme is to ask yourself "if a visitor only remembers one thing or message from this panel, I want that one thing to be _____" (Veverka 1994, 6).

- "a singular statement that captures the meaning that we hope will be retained in a visitor's psyche as a result of all the colorful facts a skilled interpreter incorporates into her/his talk, tour exhibit or web site" (Ham 2003, 3).

According to Ham (2003), the facts themselves are relatively unimportant—it's the theme or "big idea" that interpreters should try to get across to visitors. For this reason, your themes need to be strong, provocative, and designed to stick in the memory like catchy tunes. They should be inherently interesting and should entice your visitors to want to learn more about the site, feature, object, or event being interpreted. Other hallmarks of strong themes are that they present a single idea, they relate the subject to the audience, and they connect together the different pieces of information presented (Knudson et al. 1995; Regnier, Gross, and Zimmerman 1994; Serrell 1996a). Themes not only help visitors link together the ideas presented, they also provide a framework that helps interpreters decide what to focus on and what to leave out (Ham et al. 2005).

Some examples of effective themes are presented in Table 2.1—note that each presents a single idea and has been written in a format that encourages further exploration of the subject matter.

Themes are especially powerful and relevant when they make links between tangible and intangible elements. Tangible elements are things that visitors can see, touch, smell, or experience, such as historical artifacts, plants, animals, features in the environment, and works of art. Essentially, they are things visitors can assimilate through their senses (Brochu 2003). Intangible elements are symbolic; they represent beliefs and values and cannot be assimilated through the senses (Ham et al.

Table 2.1 Examples of Effective Interpretive Themes

Example of theme	Source
Most of what we know about the Universe comes from messages we read in light.	Serrell (1996a, 3)
What a swamp is good for: clean water, flood control, recreation, habitats for wildlife, natural beauty, cultural traditions.	Serrell (1996a, 3)
Manufacturing a miracle: Brooklyn and the story of penicillin	Serrell (1996a, 4)
Sharks are not what you think.	Serrell (1996a, 4)
Because they look for food in different places, many birds can live together on a small patch of water like Blackford Pond.	Carter (1997, 8)
Humans can help make this a good place for birds to live.	Carter (1997, 8)
Three kinds of frogs live in this forest, and knowing which is which could save your life.	Ham (1992, 38)
To understand Mayans, one must understand their fascination with the stars.	Ham (1992, 38)
Robert E. Lee was a famous soldier, but his personal life is poorly understood.	Ham (1992, 38)
What is a mossland?—a shallow saucer of clay holding a wet sponge of peat.	Pierssene (1999, 87)

2005). Intangible elements include concepts such as family, love, adventure, and work (Brochu 2003). Some intangible elements have been labeled "universal concepts" because they resonate with all audiences regardless of their backgrounds and experiences. These include concepts such as family, friendship, pain, work, play, love, death, beauty, and joy (Brochu and Merriman 2002). What implications does this have for designing interpretive signs and exhibits? Essentially, it suggests that if your themes link together tangible artifacts, events, and places with intangible elements (especially universal concepts), your interpretation is likely to have wide appeal and relevance.

The theme you select can have a huge impact on how the feature, object, or event is viewed by visitors. Table 2.2 illustrates how one topic can give rise to a range of possible themes.

We have already mentioned that themes need to match the interpretive objectives of the site or attraction, but how do interpreters actually develop the wording of their themes? Several common approaches are listed below:

- Adapting the questions that visitors may have about a topic or place (see Figure 2.2 for an example of themes developed for a sea lion resting area from a visitor question)
- Addressing common misconceptions held by visitors
- Describing the special and/or unique features of a place
- Developing a concept map for a topic
- Thinking of analogies and metaphors

Table 2.2 Turning One Topic into Several Interpretive Themes

Topics/subjects	Themes
Peregrine falcons (Regnier et al. 1994, 12)	➤ Falcons are uniquely adapted to preying on other birds. ➤ Hunting with falcons has been the sport of nobility for centuries. ➤ Falcon populations have suffered worldwide decline due to the use of pesticides.
Birds (Ham 1992, 35)	➤ Birds are a very interesting group of animals because of their special adaptations for flight. ➤ Native birds in this country are rapidly disappearing. ➤ Hummingbirds are a lot like helicopters. Their special wings allow them to fly backward or hover in the air. ➤ Eagles and falcons help humans. ➤ The turkey vulture fulfills the role of "garbage collector," which is an extremely important, though undervalued, ecological function. ➤ Studying how birds fly led to the invention of early airplanes. ➤ Because they're rarely seen, nocturnal birds are the subject of many superstitions and potentially threatening misconceptions.
Books	➤ Prior to the printing press, books were a sign of wealth. ➤ Popular fiction: An insight into the customs, language, and concerns of an era ➤ Books take you on a journey to another world! ➤ This manuscript represents one monk's entire life's work. ➤ Books: Portable entertainment systems!
Churches	➤ The foundations of this church were laid when William was a baby, yet he was a great-grandfather before it was completed. ➤ Churches were the social, political, and economic hub of medieval life. ➤ Beneath many abbeys and churches lie the crypts of smaller, older ones. ➤ Ghosts of past parishioners ensure this church is never empty! ➤ The stones that once formed the nave of this church now hold up the chimney in the Great Hall of Newbury Manor.
Frogs	➤ Frogs: They're not as slimy as you might think! ➤ Frogs tell us how healthy the environment is. ➤ Frogs: Nature's opera singers!

that connect a topic to the visitors' everyday life (Table 2.3 provides some analogies from a project conducted with biology students to generate analogies for basic biological concepts)

• Conducting brainstorming sessions and other creative thinking techniques

Regardless of the approach you choose, you will need to spend time reviewing, editing, and reworking your theme or package of themes until they are powerful and convey real meaning (Ham et al. 2005). The process of developing draft themes using some of these approaches is illustrated in the following pages. Table 2.3 provides some examples of designing analogies.

Table 2.3 Everyday Analogies for Biological Concepts

Biological concept	Everyday analogy
Cells	A city with a government, roads, and businesses
Genetics	Painting using the same colors to produce different artworks
Body systems	Factories processing and transporting materials
Classification	Sorting sports cards in a collection
Ecology	A cricket game

Source: Middleton (1991)

Themes and Subthemes

One of the critical characteristics of a theme is that it's the single thread that ties together the pieces of information presented in a sign or exhibit. Because it is the main underlying idea that you want visitors to take away with them, your central theme must be supported throughout the site. Brochu (2003) cites an example of an aquarium with an exhibit on the dangers of sea turtles swallowing plastic bags that fails to reinforce this theme because its gift shop items are packaged in plastic bags.

Choosing the Best Tool for the Job

Once you have established your themes and have a good understanding of the resources and opportunities available, you can begin to match messages to places, times, and types of interpretation. To demonstrate matching themes to locations and types of interpretation,

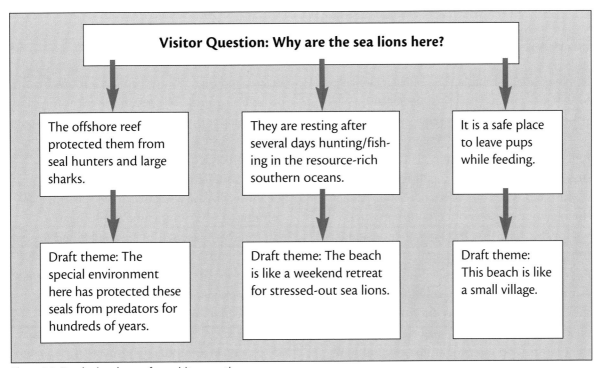

Figure 2.2. Developing themes from visitor questions

Table 2.4 Summary of Interpretive Components of the Management Plan for Noosa National Park

Level one:

Matching interpretation to the four visitor use zones

Special protection zone	Conservation zone	Conservation and recreation zone	Intensive recreation zone
Limited public use No on-site interpretation	Isolated hiking experiences Boundary and management signs only	Range of hiking activities Diversity of active recreational opportunities Interpretation signs, some interpretive displays, and self-guided interpretive trails	High levels of visitor use Visitor center and information boards

Level two:

Matching interpretation to the message and audience

Messages about not bringing domestic pets and not riding horses to be addressed through previsit information available from tour operators and local accommodation places	Messages about the park's values to be included in displays in the visitor center at the main entrance, signs at lookouts, guided activities during holidays, and presentations at the amphitheater proposed for the main entrance	Messages about minimal impact and safe hiking to be provided in a brochure available at various locations

Source: Derived from the Noosa National Park Management Plan, Queensland Parks and Wildlife Service, Australia (1993).

let's look at an example. The Management Plan for Noosa National Park in Queensland, Australia, is presented in Table 2.4.

A core element of this plan is the use of four zones. These partition visitor activities that may be incompatible, allow for a range of different types of experience, and manage the negative impacts of certain types of visitor use. The first level of the interpretation plan sets out the amount and range of interpretation to be included in each zone (summarized in the first column). Because the overall goal of having the zones is to create different types of visitor experience, the plan has no interpretation and minimal use of signs in two of the zones, with a more

extensive range of interpretive options for the other two zones. The second level of the plan involves identifying management issues that are then linked to suggested themes and interpretive activities. This phase also includes matching activities to particular locations and/or audiences (see second column). For example, an amphitheater for interpretive presentations was planned for the main entry point because this is the best location to gather together the large numbers of visitors needed for presentations to be a cost-effective interpretive technique.

The decisions made in interpretive plans are based on an understanding of the strengths and limitations associated with

Table 2.5 Advantages and Disadvantages of Signs

Advantages	Disadvantages
➤ Can be used by a large number of visitors	➤ Cannot be easily changed
➤ Can be used in just about any setting	➤ Cannot be adapted to seasonal or other regular changes
➤ Are available whenever the site is open	➤ Cannot answer questions or adapt information to specific visitors
➤ Are usually cheaper in the long run than staff	➤ Can be intrusive in some settings
➤ Can provide access to visitors who speak other languages and, if properly designed, can provide access for hearing and sight impaired visitors	➤ Must be concise and to the point, and therefore may not be suitable for complex messages
➤ Can be read by visitors at their own pace and in their own way	➤ Require effort from the visitor
➤ Are silent and, if well designed and positioned, can be unobtrusive	➤ May not be read in their entirety
➤ Provide optional interpretation—visitors can choose whether or not to access the information	➤ Have to communicate to a wide range of people

For more comparisons between signs and other media, see Aldridge (1993).

different types of interpretation. A good interpretive plan starts with the intended message and knowledge of who the likely visitors are and their characteristics and chooses the best techniques within the limits of the resources available. A good plan does not start with the technique and then decide what to say. Your first planning question should not be "What do I include in my sign or exhibit?" but "Is a sign or exhibit the best interpretive technique for this purpose and site?"

Interpretive Signs and Exhibits: The Pros and Cons

Most interpretive signs and exhibits are expensive and are designed and constructed to be in place for long periods of time. Before rushing into the design phase, it is important to consider whether signs are in fact the best interpretive option for your particular purpose. Table 2.5 lists some of the main

advantages and disadvantages of using signs in interpretation. Perhaps the greatest advantage of installing signs is that they provide a cost-effective method of reaching large audiences in settings where other interpretation may not be possible, practical, or affordable. The main drawback of using signs to convey interpretive messages is that they have limited flexibility in terms of making changes, updating information, and providing a wide range of alternative messages.

The relative inflexibility of interpretive signs and the cost of signage materials highlight the importance of considering pros and cons of signage early in the interpretive planning stages. As part of this process, you also should address the issue of ongoing maintenance. Regardless of the material chosen, ongoing maintenance is *vital* if signs are to remain vibrant and effective. Poorly maintained signs are difficult to read and give visitors the impression that you don't value your message or their experience (Merriman

Their brilliant, scarlet colour
comes from their food
which is rich in carotene
(a colouring chemical also
found in carrots). In the
wild, they get carotene from
crabs. At the Aquarium,
they eat the shrimp-like,
carotene-rich krill.

The ibises visit the ponds only
when it's time to eat.

Figure 2.3. Signs need care and attention.

and Brochu 2005). In fact, in some cases they may even be seen as having a negative environmental impact. Allocating someone early in the planning process to clean, repair, and replace signs will ensure that you don't send visitors these negative messages.

Do Interpretive Signs and Exhibits Actually Work?

In situations where personal guides cannot be provided, or where the aim is to encourage visitors to be proactive in exploring and understanding a site or topic, there is nothing better than a good interpretive sign! With careful thought and placement, signs can be used for most interpretive purposes. To illustrate with an example, visitors to the Great Barrier Reef cause considerable damage to the coral if they stand on it. Reducing this risk requires raising visitors' awareness of their behavior and the damage it inflicts. It also requires the provision of some physical design solution, such as floating stations where visitors can rest and view the coral without having to stand on it. Obviously, installing signs on the reef itself is not an option. However, signs prominently displayed on tour boats and beaches encouraging visitors not to stand on the coral and to use the floating stations instead are a useful reminder of the environmental damage that visitors can cause if they are not careful.

In some settings a sign may be the only appropriate interpretive option. For example, in very remote parks or places with few staff, signs can provide valuable information that would otherwise not be available. However, if the material required is lengthy (such as detailed minimal impact guidelines for hiking and camping in wilderness), it may be too much to expect hikers to remember all the information from a sign in the parking lot or at the trailhead. This was clearly demonstrated in a study by Hughes and Morrison-Saunders (2002) that compared visitor learning before and after installation of trailside signs along the Tree Top Walk in Western Australia. The walk had originally been designed using a minimalist approach, with signage restricted to the central kiosk area and the access jetty. Visitor surveys in 1999 revealed that visitors wanted more trailside signs, and that many were frustrated at not being able to recall information from trailhead signs while on the walk itself. Three new signs reiterating the messages of the kiosk signs were installed and evaluated. Although visitor knowledge did not improve—possibly due to the fact that the information itself had not changed—visitors' perceptions of the site as a learning environment did. The authors concluded that having information "on tap" rather than having to recall information from trailhead signs enhanced the visitor experience, particularly for repeat visitors who were already familiar with the Tree Top Walk experience.

Interpretive signs and exhibits are also particularly useful for places of quiet contemplation (e.g., religious sites, cemeteries, gardens); sites where there are alternative uses (e.g., schools, courthouses, theaters); and sites where the level of noise makes other forms of interpretation, such as talks and audiovisual presentations, impractical (e.g., factories, building sites).

Signs are popular with visitors because they are permanently accessible, are generally available to visitors free of charge, and can be read in as much or little detail as preferred. In many places visitors both expect and want interpretive signs. For instance, a survey of more than 1,200 tourists to the rain forest parks of tropical North Queensland, Australia, found that interpretive signs were the third most desired facility after basic trails and restrooms. Indeed, signs were even regarded as more important than boardwalks, picnic shelters, and grills (Moscardo 2001).

A study conducted by Light (1995) at four ancient monuments in Wales found that the most commonly used form of interpretation was outdoor interpretive panels or signs. Ninety-eight percent of the visitors surveyed stated that they had read at least some of an outdoor panel, compared with 87 percent who went to an interpretive exhibition on-site and 72 percent who used an audio tour. Likewise, a study of visitors to the Skyrail Rainforest Cableway in northern Australia found 80 percent of visitors went on a boardwalk with interpretive signs, 62 percent went to the interpretive center, and 39 percent spoke with a ranger or took a guided walk (Moscardo and Woods 1998). In a similar study of visitors to Flinders Chase National Park in South Australia, 95 percent of the visitors said they read an interpretive sign, 89 percent went to the visitor center, 25 percent took a guided walk, and 19 percent attended a ranger slide show (Greenwood et al. 2000). Similar patterns have been found in wildlife viewing. For example, Woods (2001) asked visitors to a wildlife sanctuary to nominate their preferred options for interpretation about the animals on display. Interpretive signs were the second most popular option after guides, and were regarded as preferable to simply watching the animals themselves.

There is a widespread belief that people won't or don't read much of the text that is presented in interpretive signs or panels. According to Falk and Dierking (1992), a large body of research indicates that the average time visitors spend reading a sign is ten seconds or less. However, studies conducted by McManus (1989) have challenged this assumption. Instead of traditional methods of observation, McManus used microphones to record visitors' conversations at various panels in museum exhibitions. This approach revealed that visitors were reading even when they did not appear to be doing so. She surmised that visitors often begin reading a sign or panel as they approach it. Furthermore, she observed that visitors were selective in what they read, choosing pieces that looked interesting or appealing, similar to diners at a buffet. This selective reading behavior has also been reported by other researchers (e.g., Graf 1994; Serrell 1996a).

Research by Graf (1994) at the Natural History Museum in London also suggested that the propensity to read text may depend on the composition of the visitor group. Groups with children were fairly selective in their reading, had animated discussions about the displays, and were highly likely to use interactive exhibits. Couples did not engage in conversation as much, but did tend to read each sign comprehensively. People on their own focused on text rather than the objects or activities, and read in detail. Groups of adults read the least of all groups studied, and also tended to spend the least amount of time in front of exhibits. These findings were supported by McManus (1994), who found that those on their own spent more time reading labels than those in pairs or groups. Likewise, observation studies in the Queensland Museum in Australia by Packer and Ballantyne (2005) revealed that solitary visitors spent 37 percent of their time reading text, whereas pairs spent only 25 percent of their time reading.

Similar patterns of selective reading have been obtained by asking visitors to report on their own reading behavior. Wolf and Smith (1993) interviewed visitors to various sections of the Smithsonian Institution in Washington, D.C. Respondents reported that they usually read the signs or labels in museums and that these were important in helping them to understand the displays. Likewise, in Light's (1995) study of visitation to Welsh monuments, 48 percent of visitors reported that they stopped at all panels, 38 percent stopped at most, and 13 percent stopped at some of the panels. When asked how much of the text they had read, 52 percent reported reading all the text, 45 percent said they had read some of the text, and only 3 percent reported reading virtually nothing.

Thus, it seems that most visitors read something, but very few read everything. However, this does not mean that we as interpreters are failures, nor does it suggest that we should reduce the number and length of signs. Rather, it indicates that there

are a variety of reading behaviors and learning preferences among visitors, and that this variation should be taken into account when designing signs and exhibits. Also be aware that a range of external factors, such as the amount of time visitors have, motives for the visit, nature of the exhibit, and visitors' interest in the topic, will also influence how much is read. These issues are taken up in more detail in chapters five and six, where we discuss how to write and present text that visitors will understand.

Few studies have compared the effectiveness of signs with other forms of interpretation; however, the existing evidence suggests that signs can be effective interpretive tools, although some signs are better than others. The fact that signs are one of the most commonly used interpretive tools suggests that providers believe they are an

Table 2.6 Interest in, or Satisfaction with, Different Interpretive Options

Study	Interpretive options	High interest or satisfaction
Light (1995) Welsh monuments	Audio tours	87%
	Outdoor panels/signs	50%
	Exhibition	33%
Moscardo and Woods (1998) Skyrail Rainforest Cableway	Interpretive center	77%
	Talks with rangers	70%
	Boardwalk with interpretive signs	65%
	Ranger-led tour	65%
	Trip brochure	61%
Greenwood et al. (2000) Flinders Chase National Park	Talking to staff	30%
	Interpretive signs	25%
	Guided walks	20%
	Ranger slide shows	20%
	Visitor center	17%
Ham and Weiler (2000) Panama Protected Areas	Explanations by area staff	84%
	Presentation and exhibits	84%
	Visitor centers	78%
	Brochures	74%
	Maps	74%

effective method of communicating with visitors. Several visitor studies have also assessed visitor satisfaction with different interpretive options. Results are presented in Table 2.6, and indicate that although signs weren't the best option, in all four cases they were not significantly less preferred than the other forms of interpretation.

Light measured level of interest, and figures reported are for visitors rating the options as very interesting.

Moscardo and Woods asked for a rating of satisfaction on a scale from 0 to 10, and the figures reported are for visitors giving the option a score of 8 or higher.

Greenwood et al. asked for a rating of satisfaction on a 4-point scale from "not at all" to "very satisfied," and the figures reported are for visitors giving a "very satisfied" rating.

Ham and Weiler measured satisfaction on a 5-point scale from "very dissatisfied" to "very satisfied."

Jacobson (1988) took a different approach and tested visitors' knowledge after they had hiked a trail in a Malaysian national park. In this study, four groups were compared: a control group who hiked a trail without any interpretation, those who were accompanied by a guide, those who went with a booklet, and those who hiked the trail after signs were installed. The results showed that all three interpretive options were more effective (as measured by visitors' posthike knowledge) than no interpretation at all. The highest knowledge scores were for the guided hike, with signs and booklets having a similar score. Olsen, Bowman, and Roth (1984) also found that signs improve visitor knowledge. Their research was conducted in nature reserves in the United States and revealed that there was a significant improvement in knowledge of, and positive attitudes toward, conservation when signs were available for visitors. The signs were not, however, as effective as interpretive talks or brochures.

Johnson and Swearingen (1992) also reported positive environmental attitudes and behavior as a result of reading signage. These researchers found that the installation of trailside signs informing people about the negative impacts of walking off trails was associated with a significant reduction in this behavior. Likewise, Borun and Miller (1980) studied a participatory science experiment with and without a sign and concluded that the sign improved visitor understanding and encouraged them to participate. It appears that although signs are not necessarily the most effective form of interpretation, they can nevertheless have a substantial impact on visitors' attitudes, knowledge, and behavior, and are far better than no interpretation at all.

Key Points

Interpretive signs enhance the quality of visitors' experiences and can influence how they behave in the interpretive setting. Signs enable interpreters to convey the significance of objects, events, and/or sites, and are an integral aspect of modern tourism and leisure experiences. Interpretive signs help to protect vulnerable sites by informing visitors of appropriate behavior, fostering concern about the environment, and in extremely fragile or inaccessible areas, providing substitute experiences.

Planning interpretive signs involves the following three basic steps:

1. Defining the objectives of your proposed interpretation, specifically:
   - What is special about your site, event, and/or object?
   - What are your visitor management issues?
   - What are the constraints of your setting for interpretation?
   - Who is your expected audience?
2. Translating your objectives into workable themes

3. Selecting the best interpretive technique for your particular site and purpose

Interpretive signs are not always the most cost-effective and appropriate form of interpretation. The advantages and disadvantages of using signage as the main vehicle for your interpretive message should be carefully considered prior to design and installation.

Chapter 3

LOOK AT ME!
Getting Visitors' Attention

An interpretive sign or exhibit can be effective only if it attracts attention. Visitors won't see signs and exhibits that are hidden or poorly positioned, nor will they read signs that fail to grab their attention or stimulate their curiosity. We start this chapter with a discussion about the placement of interpretive signs. Following this, we will integrate research about attracting attention with what is known about sign effectiveness to produce a set of guidelines for designing interpretive signs that attract visitors' attention and encourage them to read further.

Figure 3.1. Sign placement is important—you need to balance easy to read with unobtrusive.

Location, Location, Location!

The two basic rules for effective sign placement are to put the sign where people are most likely to see it and where it can be directly connected to the object or feature it interprets (Bucy 2005). The first step in determining the best location for signs is to have some understanding of how visitors

move through your site. When visitors enter an interpretive setting, they are physically and psychologically "fresh" and ready to explore. This doesn't last forever, though—as the visit progresses, people become mentally and physically fatigued. Consequently, the number of signs they read as well as the time and effort they take to absorb each sign's content steadily decreases. Not surprisingly, signs placed close to exits are typically the least viewed because visitors are not only tired, they are also distracted by the exit itself (Dean 1994).

Observational studies of families in two natural history museums (Falk and Dierking 1992) revealed that visitors tend to divide their time according to the following pattern:

- A familiarization phase lasting three to ten minutes
- A concentrated viewing phase that involves intense reading and interaction with exhibits. This lasts between twenty-five and thirty minutes.
- A selective viewing phase during which visitors scan signs and exhibits, only stopping at those which particularly spark their interest. This lasts a further thirty to forty minutes.
- A five- to ten-minute departure phase that involves visits to the gift shop and restrooms

What implications do these patterns of visitor behavior have for placement of important messages? First, signs and exhibits encountered at the beginning of the visit, such as at the entrance to galleries, museums, or the start of trails, are likely to attract the most attention. Similarly, if the visitor attraction is multistoried, exhibits located on the first floor are the ones most likely to be read (Falk and Dierking 1992). This implies that if you have messages that are critical to the understanding and appreciation of the topic/event/site being interpreted, you should place them "up front" to maximize their chances of being read and absorbed. Second, in general, the farther a sign is from the entrance, the less likely people are to read it. Consequently, messages and topics that are less important or do not have universal appeal would be better positioned farther from the entrance. This does not discriminate against visitors with an interest in these topics, as they would be attracted to the sign regardless of its position, but it does mean that those who skip the signs are not missing vital content.

But exactly *where* should signs be placed to be most obvious? One way of identifying where visitors go and what they look at is to examine patterns of wear and tear throughout your site (Brochu 2003). Worn carpets in front of exhibits and signs, well-worn paths, and patches in lawns indicate the features of your site that are attracting visitors' attention. If you place them perpendicular to visitors' line of approach, your signs will be more likely to attract attention than if you place them parallel to pathways (Korn 1988; McIntosh 1996). Indeed, a study of visitors and signs in a display area for polar bears and sea lions at the Denver Zoo revealed that less than 20 percent of the people who passed signs placed parallel to the walkway stopped to read them (Birney 1993).

In another study of zoo visitors, this time at the Brookfield Zoo in Chicago, Serrell (1981) reported an increase of 26 percent in the number of visitors looking at an interpretive sign when it was moved from an

Figure 3.2. Think about where the reader will be looking.

adjacent wall to directly above the animal exhibit. However, she does sound a warning against placing signs too high, stating that visitors often fail to notice signs that are more than six or seven feet (two meters) off the ground. In a similar study, Arndt and his colleagues (1993) shifted a sign from an adjacent wall to the center of a viewing area for a lion display at the Milwaukee County Zoo in Wisconsin. Their observations revealed that the number of people reading the sign increased from 5 percent to 80 percent and that the time spent looking at the lions increased from an average of 75 seconds to 104 seconds.

Figures 3.3 and 3.4 show the number of visitors stopping at displays in a temporary exhibition on telecommunications staged at the Museum of Victoria in Australia, which was studied by one of the authors (Moscardo 1999). The two figures show that regardless of which direction visitors turned when they entered the hall, they were much more likely to stop at displays positioned closer to the center of their line of vision. The Strowger Exchange, for example, was an interactive exhibit that had both sound and movement and therefore was able to catch some visitors' attention even if placed off the main path. Despite this, it was still less successful in attracting visitors who approached from the left than for those who approached from the right.

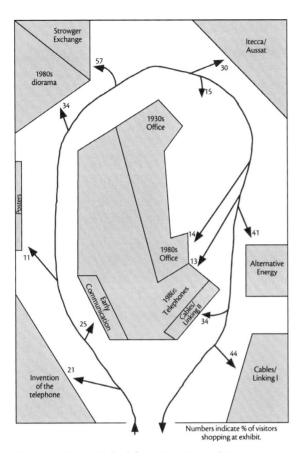

Figure 3.3. What did the left-turning visitors do?

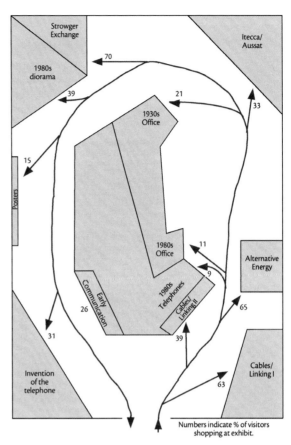

Figure 3.4. What did the right-turning visitors do?

Locating signs within visitors' line of vision is also important when labeling objects or features of the environment. Signs need to be within easy viewing distance of the interpreted object, as visitors prefer not to move back and forth between the interpretation and its topic. Consequently, signs placed directly next to the object or feature being interpreted are more likely to be read than those with keyed legends that are placed farther away. Likewise, if you are asking visitors to compare two objects, both of them should be visible from where the visitor is reading the sign (Bucy 2005; Serrell 1996a). It is also important to check that directions for viewing interpreted objects or features are correct. For example, if your sign directs visitors to look at a particular object on their right, it is imperative that this be where the object is actually located (Serrell 1996a). Surprisingly, this is not always the case.

Visitors' perspective of objects or features is also critical when designing signs that include illustrations. If, for instance, your sign includes an illustration of an object from the side, do your visitors also have a side view of the object? If your sign discusses the geological formation of a valley or the structure of a building, does the accompanying diagram illustrate features that are clearly visible and easily distinguishable when standing in front of the sign?

Research indicates that many visitors do not view exhibits in sequence (Falk and Dierking 1992). So if your signs are organized in chronological order, or if comprehension of one sign requires visitors to have read a previous one, this needs to be clearly stated at the beginning. One author visited an exhibition on the history of rock and roll, but because the exhibit was not titled as such, nor were there directions about which was the entrance and which the exit, she

Figure 3.5. Is the sign too close to its subject?

simply followed other visitors. The end result was that the whole group wandered through the exhibit in the wrong direction, failing to realize that it was a historical account until they reached the final display summarizing the major historical milestones. Their comprehension of the exhibit material and enjoyment of the experience were severely hampered by encountering the information in a "nonsensical" order, and many promptly turned around and went through the whole display again in the correct order to make sense of the experience. The message is clear: If the order in which signs are read is important, position them accordingly and install an introductory sign alerting visitors to this fact.

If you are catering to visitors who predominantly read from left to right, signs should be organized to facilitate a left-to-right pattern of eye and body movement.

Paragraphs and signs will "flow" when read from left to right, but if visitors get to the bottom right corner of one sign then have to move to their left to read the next, the whole experience becomes disjointed. Obviously, this is a language-dependent issue, and if catering mainly to Asian visitors, for example, the left-to-right, top-to-bottom convention will need to be adjusted (Dean 1994). The reading habits of the target audience are important considerations for all interpretive sites, as "unnatural" positioning of signs has the potential to create traffic flow problems, further disrupting the reading experience. For example, the National Atomic Museum in Albuquerque, New Mexico, has a display in which the reader has to move from right to left to read the panels. Visitors entering this display space automatically start reading the left panel and only find they are reading out of sequence by the time they get to the third panel.

The placement of signs is also important in outdoor settings. In very large sites, such as parks and zoos and along trails, there tend to be natural stopping points and common decision points. These include forks in the trail, lookouts, picnic and seating areas, playgrounds, and "hubs" around which display cabinets, enclosures, and other features can be arranged. If possible, signs should be located close to these to maximize visibility and increase the likelihood of them being read (Trapp et al. 1994). The diagrams in Figures 3.6 and 3.7 are from the interpretive plan for the Eastern Lake Ontario Sand Dune and Wetland Park. These illustrate how to place interpretive signs at points directly in visitors' line of sight as they approach, and at points where visitors are most likely to stop.

You might have noticed that in Figure 3.7 there is no interpretive sign planned for the proposed lookout over Deer Creek. One of the exceptions to our rule about placing a

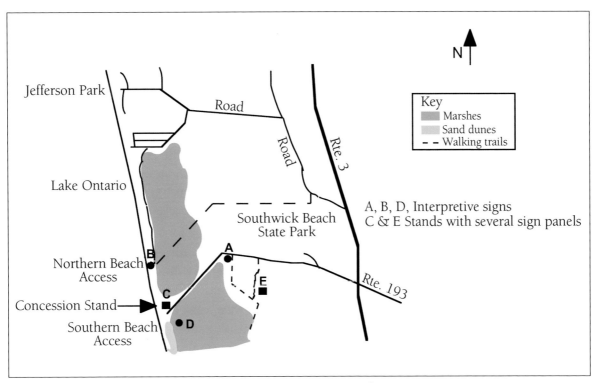

Figure 3.6. Some ideas about where signs should go (Adapted from Earnest 1994)

sign in the center of the visitors' line of vision is when such a sign may interfere with the view of the feature, object, or vista that is being interpreted. Indeed, in some places it may be intrusive to place a sign in the center of the view, particularly if it is one that visitors would like to contemplate for a while or to photograph (Korn 1988; Trapp et al. 1994). In these cases, place signs within easy

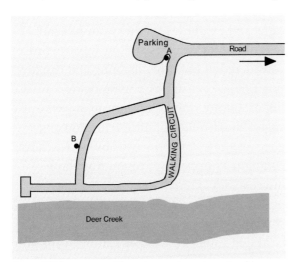

Figure 3.7. Some more ideas about where signs should go (Adapted from Earnest 1994)

viewing distance and clearly match the information to the feature(s) being described. Regardless of where they are positioned, signs can be very intrusive if they do not blend in with their surroundings. This particularly applies to natural settings— nature should still dominate, no matter how important the interpretive message (Gunn 1994). Features such as paths, gardens, and outdoor seating areas should all be designed to support your central theme and interpretive signs and exhibits (Merriman and Brochu 2005). A good example of this can be found at the Singapore Zoo, where "jungle-themed" restrooms have sinks that are open to the sky and surrounded by lush foliage.

As with most things, though, there is a fine line between blending in and disappearing altogether. Hughes and Morrison-Saunders (2002) report that many visitors to the Ancient Empire walk in Western Australia were surprised when asked about their impressions of signs embedded into board-walks. The reason for their surprise—they hadn't even noticed there were any signs! The lesson to learn here is that we need to find a balance between preserving the integrity of the landscape and providing signage that attracts attention and enhances visitors' experiences.

How Low Can You Go?

Several authors have suggested that the center of the sign should be placed at adult eye level (Korn 1988). Others argue that this recommendation ignores the fact that many settings attract children and people in wheelchairs. A better alternative may be to place the sign lower, but angle it upward so that everyone finds it easy to see.

Too Many Visitors Spoil the View

Positioning signage also requires careful consideration of the numbers of visitors expected at any given time. McManus (1998) provides a detailed discussion of the problems visitors face in concentrating on interpretation when they feel crowded. She argues that planners need to make paths and spaces big enough so that visitors don't feel crowded and can focus on the interpretive content. Another consideration is that visitors are often uncomfortable if others are waiting, and may not read as much of the sign as they would have had it been less crowded. Indeed, in areas with a definite traffic flow, it has been observed that families tend to move on when a new group arrives, even if they haven't actually finished viewing the exhibit. Family groups also tend to avoid displays that are crowded or surrounded by other visitors (Kropf 1989). If your aim is to hold the attention of groups or families for long periods, you need to create sufficient space around the interpretive signs and exhibits to accommodate everyone.

The importance of reducing crowding and optimizing traffic flow is particularly evident in narrow or confined areas. If there is a definite direction of movement through these areas, detailed or complex signage is not recommended, as visitors trying to absorb the content of the sign are likely to create bottlenecks. If you do want to provide detailed interpretation or instructions, place these away from the main traffic flows in areas where visitors can easily stop and read (Knudson et al. 1995). The same principle applies to outdoor signage such as trails and highway information signs—there must be sufficient space for people and vehicles to pull off the main routes without creating safety hazards. If visitors are expected to get out of their vehicles to read the signs, there must also be sufficient space for pedestrian movement (Gunn 1994).

Figure 3.8 presents a site plan showing visitor flow paths past an open animal exhibit plus possible locations for an interpretive sign. Taking into account what you have learned about attracting people's attention through sign placement, which of the six points do you think is the best location for an interpretive sign? (See the end of this chapter for some suggestions.)

Let There Be Light!

Sign placement also needs to take into account sources of light and how this affects signs and exhibits. Lighting is an integral part of indoor exhibits and must be carefully considered in both the planning and installation phases. When positioning lights it is important not only to illuminate objects and signs, but also to minimize reflection and glare, as these can reduce visibility. The most common sources of reflection from both internal and external lighting are glass, polished surfaces, floor coverings, and other shiny materials.

Light sources are either natural, artificial, or a combination of the two. Some natural lighting is generally desirable, although this

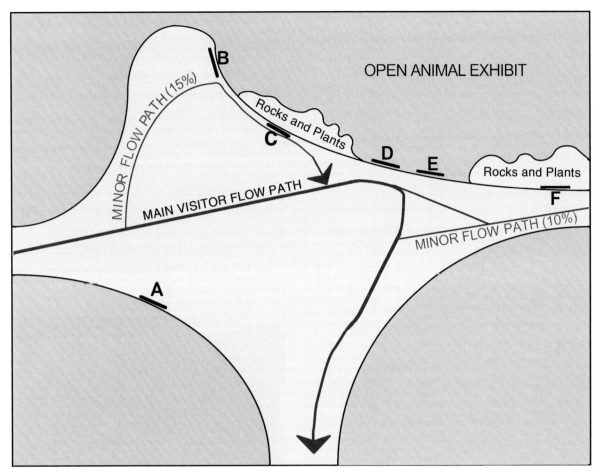

Figure 3.8. Where is the best place for an interpretive sign?

often needs to be carefully controlled through the use of blinds, curtains, or screens. In some cases, however, natural light is too bright, and can even damage displays and signage (Bligh and Brooker 1992). Another drawback of relying on natural light is that it tends to be highly variable from hour to hour and day to day. This may affect the "ambience" of your interpretive facility as well as the visibility of exhibits and signs (Bligh and Brooker 1992; Helms and Belcher 1991).

Obviously, if signs and displays are outdoors, there is little choice but to rely on natural sources of light. In these situations, careful consideration needs to be given to the position of the sun at different times of the day. Looking at a feature or sign with bright sunlight behind it is uncomfortable and needs to be taken into account when designing your

interpretive experiences. It may be that some trails are best traveled in a clockwise direction in the morning and counterclockwise in the afternoon. If so, your visitors should be told this at the start of the trail (Pierssene 1999). Also keep in mind that signs that face bright

Figure 3.9. Reflecting on reflection

sunlight need to be constructed from materials that are nonreflective and durable enough to resist fading. To further enhance readability, signs in bright sunlight should have light-colored lettering on dark backgrounds, whereas those in shaded areas are easier to read if they have dark lettering on light backgrounds (Trapp et al. 1994).

Sunlight and natural lighting tend to be highly variable, but sources of artificial lighting are constant, easy to adjust, and can be used to illuminate a range of displays and spaces. There are two broad categories of artificial lighting: fluorescent and incandescent. Fluorescent lighting is usually used for general illumination because it is soft and does not cast shadows. Care must be taken to install a sufficient number of lights, however, as low levels of fluorescent lighting can make rooms appear dark and confined (Bligh and Brooker 1992). Incandescent lighting transmits beams of light that can be focused on signs or specific elements of exhibits. These lights can be filtered, dimmed, or softened and are available in a wide range of types and sizes. Their main disadvantage is that high-voltage types generate levels of heat that can damage exhibits. This can be overcome, however, by installing low-voltage incandescent bulbs, which are expensive to purchase but relatively cheap to operate (Bligh and Brooker 1992).

Appropriate and correctly positioned lighting enables visitors to see objects by creating contrasts within the objects and between the objects and their backgrounds. However, if you install the wrong type of lighting or place lights in the wrong position, visitors will find it difficult to view your signs and exhibits. Some common problems listed by Miles et al. (1988) include the following:

- Accent lighting creates glare, making it difficult and sometimes impossible to see anything.
- Diffuse lighting can cause reflections that impede vision.
- Spotlights create reflections on shiny surfaces such as glass, metal, and printing ink.
- Widely different and rapidly changing levels of illumination create visual fatigue.

You should also check that indoor lighting does not create shadows that affect the legibility of your signs. Although it is common practice to print text on transparent surfaces, if the indoor lighting creates shadows, the text becomes virtually impossible to read.

Figure 3.10. Think about shadows so your visitors don't have to.

It must also be noted that people need time to adjust to differences in light levels. Although initial adaptation takes only twenty to thirty seconds, full adaptation can take as long as thirty minutes (Shaw 2002a). The implications for indoor exhibits are important—if your visitors are coming from outdoors into dimly lit exhibits, they will need a series of "staging" areas that have progressively lower levels of light to enable their eyes to adapt comfortably and ensure that the exhibits and signs don't appear dark and gloomy (Shaw 2002a).

HEY YOU—YES, YOU— READ ME!
Methods of Attracting Attention

Visitors won't read your sign if they don't notice it exists. As designers, we need to create signs that grab visitors' attention and entice them to read further. We can do this by incorporating the following characteristics into signs and exhibits:

- Extreme things, particularly very large, very loud, and very colorful things
- Contrast, particularly if this makes elements stand out from their background
- Unexpected and surprising things
- Text that speaks directly to visitors
- Movement

(See Moscardo 1996 and 1998 for more details.)

Table 3.1 provides a summary of research evaluating the effectiveness of interpretive displays and demonstrates how these characteristics attract visitor attention in tourism and recreation settings.

Some of these elements are mentioned in Ham's "Knockan Theory" (2002), which states that the closer topics or elements are to the left-hand side of Figure 3.11, the more likely they will create interest among visitors. Thus, interpretation focusing on topics closely related to humans (e.g., other people, mammals) generally attracts more attention than interpretation of inanimate objects such as rocks; interpretation about dangerous topics such as hurricanes generates more interest than interpretation of safe things such as clouds; and so on.

Catchy Titles and Other Tricks

The principles presented in Table 3.1 have been combined with research in the areas of psychology, tourism, and education to produce the following guidelines for designing signs that attract visitors' attention:

Table 3.1 Display Features That Attract Visitor Attention

Principle	Interpretive features	Study
Extreme things	Larger type in titles	Thompson and Bitgood (1988) Arndt et al. (1993)
Contrast	Color in titles	Wolf and Smith (1993) Arndt et al. (1993)
Unexpected/surprising things	Three-dimensional features on signs Provocative headings that use puns or other plays on words	Birney (1993) Rand (1985)
Directly addressing the individual	Titles asking a question	Serrell (1981) Kanel and Tamir (1991) Hartley and Trueman (1983)
Movement	Signs with visible interactive elements such as sliding panels	Birney (1993) Arndt et al. (1993)

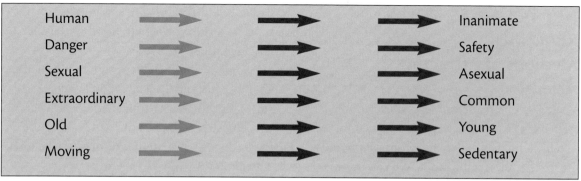

Figure 3.11. Things on the left matter to us all.

1. Use larger type for titles.

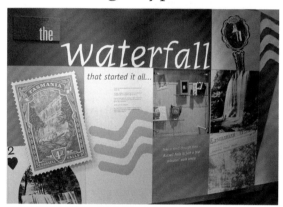

Figure 3.12. When it comes to size, a bigger title is usually better.

2. Use color or another means of contrast.

Even if they don't have a preference for bright hues, people's eyes are naturally drawn to areas and objects of bright color. Consequently, bright colors are often used to attract attention and can also be used to trigger mood associations. For example, titles written in large red letters suggest that the interpretation is likely to be dynamic, interactive, controversial, or stimulating. Those in more subdued, muted colors suggest a more passive visitor experience (Dean 1994). We discuss this issue in more detail in the next chapter.

3. Add three-dimensional features.

4. Use questions, analogies, or unexpected provocative statements.

Visitors will be attracted to signs that are headed by intentionally intriguing titles. Compare the two titles "Extinct Species" and "Dead as a Dodo"—both mean the same thing, but the second is much more appealing than the first. Your titles should be short (no more than ten words) and serve to thematically orient visitors (Dean 1994; Museums Australia 1998). Good titles fire the visitor's imagination, stimulate curiosity, and create the mood of the whole sign. They often include quotes, common expressions, metaphors, alliteration, provocative questions, idioms, and other clever turns of phrase. It is also common practice to parody familiar phrases or sayings—much as modern advertising does. Table 3.2 illustrates some titles designed to attract visitor attention.

As an alternative, signs can be headed by a provocative statement or "interpretive hook" that performs the same function as a title. For example, Pearce (1991) describes an Egyptian exhibition that started with the following poem:

Table 3.2 Examples of How to Make Titles Catchier

Original	Improved version
The Importance of the Cicada's Call	Cicadas: What's All the Noise About?
Life One Hundred Years Ago	Let's Go Back to 1907—What Would You Miss the Most?
Tidal Currents Brought This Sand up from the Ocean Floor	Walking on the Bottom of the Sea?
Giraffes: Giants of the African Plains	All Creatures Great and Tall: Welcome to the Giraffe's World!
Water's Role in the Earth's Survival	Survival Water: The Key to Life on Earth
Outback Australia	Sheep, Sheds, and Sheilas: Life on the Australian Outback
Noisy Pittas Clean Up the Rain Forest	Noisy Pittas: Rain Forest Trash Collectors
The Australian Way of Life	"Firing Up the Barbie": Australians Kick Back
Fire Was an Important Tool for Early Humans	Home Is Where the Hearth Is
Flying Foxes Fly More Than Sixty Miles a Night Looking for Food	Flying Foxes Spend All Night Looking for Food Now That's Hungry!
The Role of Sun in a Lizard's Survival	Why Do Lizards Lie in the Sun?

I lived in scandal and I died in sin
That's what the world is interested in …

This poem has the effect of setting the scene as well as arousing visitors' curiosity.

Be careful if you decide to use humor in your signs and exhibits, as it is highly subjective. Puns are generally the safest form; carefully worded riddles and witticisms are also good choices. Jokes that ridicule individuals

**Attention All Arctic
Ground Squirrels**

WARNING!

Refuse all handouts from humans. They mean well but their food will make you slow and fat … easy bear bait. Revert to natural foods for your own survival. Do not accept human handouts.

(Adapted from Knudson et al. 2003)

from particular ethnic, social, or religious backgrounds are likely to offend visitors and should be avoided at all costs (Beck and Cable 2002). Humor is often used to send serious messages to visitors.

5.Add movement or interactive components to your sign.

The design of hands-on interactive displays and signs will be discussed in more detail in chapter four; however, at this point it is important to state that you should not include interactive elements simply to attract attention. Rather, they should be used only if they directly connect to the interpretive material and help to further visitors' understanding of the topic being discussed.

Key Points

To be effective, signs must be positioned within visitors' line of vision and close to the

Figure 3.13. Getting interactive

features/objects/landscapes being described. If signs need to be read in a particular order, they should be positioned to facilitate this. Natural stopping areas (e.g., lookouts) and common decision points (e.g., forks in the trail) are particularly effective locations for outdoor signs. The issues of sign height, expected visitor numbers, and sources of light also need to be considered when positioning signs.

Visitors tend to notice signs that have

- Extreme elements (size, color, noise)
- Contrast
- Unexpected or surprising things
- Conversational text
- Movement

Titles with the following characteristics are particularly good at attracting visitors' attention:

- Large type
- Color
- Three dimensions
- Questions, analogies, and/or provocative statements

Where Is the Best Placement for an Interpretive Sign?

There are arguments for and against most of the choices given in Figure 3.8, except for Location A. Location A is behind the line of view of visitors and would require visitors to turn completely around to see it. Locations D and E have the advantage of being directly in the line of view of the main visitor flow path and so are likely to be seen by most visitors. These would be good locations for signs with key messages. But if the signs are too large or placed too high at locations D and E, they could interfere with viewing the animals, so careful design is needed. Locations B, C, and F are unlikely to be seen by many visitors, but they could provide additional information for those who are interested enough to take the less traveled path around this exhibit area.

Chapter 4

"Stop, Look, and Listen": Keeping Visitors' Attention

Visitors are likely to read your signs if they believe their time and effort will be rewarded with interesting and relevant information. In the previous chapter we reviewed some studies demonstrating the effectiveness of different sign features for attracting visitor attention. In this chapter we discuss studies that have identified properties of signs that encourage visitors to read beyond the title.

Striking a Balance: Effort versus Reward

Several different authors have used balance models for explaining how visitors decide whether to read interpretive signs. The premise of these models is that visitors decide whether to read a sign by comparing the difficulty of reading the sign with how interesting or valuable they expect the content to be. If effort and reward seem balanced, the visitor is likely to proceed with reading. Bitgood and Patterson (1993) labeled their model a cost-benefit model, whereas Ham (1992) and Trapp et al. (1994) refer to Schraam's "fraction of selection." The latter model can be presented as follows:

$$\text{The fraction of selection} = \frac{\text{Expectation of reward}}{\text{Effort required}}$$

When expectation of reward is greater than effort required, visitors are likely to read the sign. If, however, the effort required seems high and the expectation of reward

seems low, visitors are less likely to stop and read your signs. The implication is clear—to be effective, your interpretive signs should require minimal effort to read and offer maximum rewards.

According to the principles of interpretation outlined in chapter one (reiterated in Table 4.1), features that add to a sign's interest or perceived reward value include

- information of personal relevance;
- a direct, active, conversational style; and
- content that encourages activity and allows for interaction.

Table 4.1 Principles of Effective Interpretation

- ➤ Interpretation should make a personal connection with, or be relevant to, the intended audience.
- ➤ Interpretation should encourage novel and varied experiences.
- ➤ Interpretation should be organized with clear, easy-to-follow structures.
- ➤ Interpretation should be based on a theme.
- ➤ Interpretation should engage visitors in the learning experience and encourage them to take control of their own learning.
- ➤ Interpretation should demonstrate an understanding of, and respect for, the audience.

Features that influence the ease with which a sign is read (i.e., the effort required) include

- visual characteristics of the lettering, such as typeface and size;
- line, paragraph, and overall length;
- structure and organization of text and illustrations; and
- use of color and contrast.

Ham (1992), Korn (1988), Rogers and Brown (1993), Serrell (1996a), and Trapp et al. (1994) provide reviews of reading, communication, and instructional design research. These indicate that the following features encourage people to read signage:

- Legible type
- Shorter rather than longer signs
- Text that is broken into short sentences and paragraphs, using headings and subheadings, illustrations, and the right mix or balance of illustrations, text, and white space
- Color and contrast
- Variety
- A direct conversational style using simple sentences, active verbs, and first- and second-person pronouns
- Personal relevance
- Content that encourages action on the part of the reader

The remainder of this chapter discusses each of these features in turn and provides examples of how they can be effectively incorporated into a range of interpretive signs.

First Impressions Count

Four factors that influence legibility are the size of the font; the spacing between characters, words, and lines; the typeface or font style; and the way in which capitals and italics are used.

Font Size and Type

Optimum font or type size depends partly on the distance between the reader and the sign. Obviously, the farther away the reader, the larger the font size required. Table 4.2 provides some of the standard font sizes suggested for interpretive signs in national parks.

There is some contention among researchers about whether these are appropriate in all settings. Serrell (1996a) and Dean (1994) state that for interpretive signs in museums the range for body text should be from 18 points to 36 points. They argue that visitors are not likely to read interpretive information from more than three feet (one meter) away; therefore larger type is unnecessary and can actually be difficult to read at that distance. An exception to these rules is in situations where the distance between

Table 4.2 Standard Minimum Font Sizes for Interpretive Signs

Type of Text	Distance between reader and sign	
	0–4 ft. (0–1.5 m)	4 ft.–6 ft. (1.5–2 m)
Titles	72 points	96 points
Headings	48 points	72 points
Body text	24 points	48 points
Captions for illustrations	18 points	24 points

Sources: Ham (1992, 266); Trapp et al. (1994, 11).

readers and the text varies. Then it is suggested that the font size be increased by 6 points for every nine inches (twenty centimeters) added to the *likely* distance between readers and the text.

The following activity illustrates the importance of selecting the correct font size for your interpretive setting. Try to read the text in each of the three sections in Figure 4.1 from a different distance. First, place the page about eighteen inches (fifty centimeters) away and read each section. Which size is the easiest to read? Move the page to about twenty-seven inches (seventy centimeters) away. Is this size still the easiest to read? Now move the page to about thirty-six inches (one meter) away. Which of the three can you still read? Which is the easiest?

The importance of testing your typeface with a range of visitors in the interpretive setting cannot be emphasized enough. If visitors are unable to get close enough to your sign to read it easily, they will simply walk away. Visitors will also walk away if they think your sign is going to be difficult to read. Whereas large type attracts attention, small type is often associated with textbooks and technical reports. Consequently, signs written in small type may inadvertently send the message that the content will be too technical or difficult to understand. In many cases, visitors ignore these signs altogether (Dean 1994).

Spacing

Most word-processing programs automatically adjust the spacing to be consistent with the type size used; therefore many of us do not consider this aspect of typesetting. It is, however, important that words and lines not be placed too close together, as this detracts from the appeal and legibility of the text (Borun and Miller 1980; Korn 1988; Serrell 1996a). There is also general agreement that the best line length is between forty and sixty-five characters, including spaces. This works

Look closer for traces of the wildlife the trees support—nibbled fruits, seeds in droppings, insects in fallen blossoms. (8 pts)

Look closer for traces of the wildlife the trees support—nibbled fruits, seeds in droppings, insects in fallen blossoms. (10 pts)

Look closer for traces of the wildlife the trees support—nibbled fruits, seeds in droppings, insects in fallen blossoms. (14 pts)

Figure 4.1. How easy are these to read?

out to be approximately ten words per line (Aldridge 1993; Korn 1988; Serrell 1996a). These authors also warn against writing very short lines that break up the text too much. If you go back to Figure 4.1, you'll notice that the same sentence is presented with different line lengths. The first two versions are within the recommended line lengths (a maximum of sixty-three characters for the first example, forty-nine for the second). However, the third example is too short (thirty characters), and as a result is much harder to read.

When spacing text, it is also important to consider margins. It is generally agreed that sections of text that have a flush left margin and a ragged right margin are the easiest to read and allow for standard spaces to be used between the words (Serrell 1996a; Trapp et al. 1994). Furthermore, ragged right margins make it easy to fine-tune the spacing between words so they look even. This means that designers are able to create blocks of text that look evenly spaced without having to hyphenate words in order to fit them in. Some sign writers carry words to the next line using hyphens. Serrell (1996a), however, warns against this practice, as she claims it interrupts the flow of words and "jars" the reading process. For the same reason she also recommends not splitting paragraphs across the columns. These points are illustrated in Figure 4.2. The first example has text that is spread across columns and has a flush right margin. The second illustrates paragraphs that have been contained within the same column and has a ragged right margin. Which do you find easiest to read?

Typeface

There are four basic categories of typeface:

1. Decorative typefaces are generally difficult to read. However, with care it is possible to select one of these for use in a title to create a particular effect.
2. Serif typefaces have small end strokes on the letters.
3. Sans serif typefaces do not have end strokes. These are generally the best choice if text is backlit or if a light type is used on a dark background.
4. Transitional typefaces are, as the name suggests, somewhere between serif and sans serif styles.

Unfortunately, there are few guidelines available for deciding which typeface to use. Some authors (Ham 1992; Korn 1988; Serrell 1996a) suggest using a transitional style or a commonly used style such as

Example 1

Trees growing in nutrient-poor sands are clever at fining available food. Here, roots from nearby trees zigzag up the fan palm trunks. They are feeding on nutrients released by rotting debris that collects where palm fronds branch out from the trunk.

The reason such a tall forest can grown on mere sand is hidden just below the surface. Microscopic root fungi and the trees they grow on the trees they grow on have come to a mutual help arrangement. In fact they can't live without each other.

Trees are slow on nutrient uptake—a distinct disadvantage where nutrients are rapidly leached from the soils. In this symbiotic arrangement the root fungi absorb soil nutrients, transferring them to the tree. In return the tree supplies the fungi with sugar.

Example 2

Trees growing in nutrient-poor sands are clever at fining available food. Here, roots from nearby trees zigzag up the fan palm trunks. They are feeding on nutrients released by rotting debris that collects where palm fronds branch out from the trunk.

The reason such a tall forest can grown on mere sand is hidden just below the surface. Microscopic root fungi and the trees they grow on the trees they grow on have come to a mutual help arrangement. In fact they can't live without each other.

Trees are slow on nutrient uptake—a distinct disadvantage where nutrients are rapidly leached from the soils. In this symbiotic arrangement the root fungi absorb soil nutrients, transferring them to the tree. In return the tree supplies the fungi with sugar.

Figure 4.2. Be careful where you decide to split the text.

- Times Roman (serif),
- Bodoni Book (serif),
- **Helvetica** (sans serif), or
- Stone (transitional).

Others argue for using the typeface that best fits the theme of the interpretation.

Despite the lack of widely accepted guidelines, there are some things that should clearly be avoided. Sans serif styles are easier to read from a distance and so are often used in highway and warning signs (Korn 1988). However, sans serif styles can create problems if the words are compressed—they become too narrow and tall:

Don't squish up the words.

Alternatively, serif styles are difficult to read if the words are too stretched out:

Don't stretch out the words.

Using Capitals and Italics

Italics are difficult to read and should be used with caution. They are, however, particularly useful in short phrases to emphasize important points. Text written completely in capitals gives the impression that the information is being shouted, and can be tiring to read. It will also require considerably more space than a sign with a mixture of upper- and lowercase

Figure 4.4. It's good to mix things up a little.

> *Sandpaper figs can grow to a height of 10 meters and are usually found near sources of fresh water. Aborigines used the rough fig leaves for sanding down timber and ate its sweet red fruit throughout the early summer.*

> SANDPAPER FIGS CAN GROW TO A HEIGHT OF 10 METERS AND ARE USUALLY FOUND NEAR SOURCES OF FRESH WATER. ABORIGINES USED THE ROUGH FIG LEAVES FOR SANDING DOWN TIMBER AND ATE ITS SWEET RED FRUIT THROUGHOUT THE EARLY SUMMER.

> SANDPAPER FIGS
> Sandpaper figs can grow to a height of 10 meters and are usually found near sources of fresh water. *Aborigines used the rough fig leaves for sanding down timber* and ate its sweet red fruit throughout the early summer.

Figure 4.3. Which of these is the most appealing?

lettering. Figure 4.3 presents the same paragraph in three formats—all italics, all capitals, and a mixture of the two. Note that the text in capitals takes up the most space. Which version do you find easiest to read?

Short and Sweet

Visitors prefer and are more likely to read signs that they believe have fewer words. An effective method of making signs appear short is to include only two or three topics or pieces of information per sign. In 1993 Bitgood and Patterson reported on a study of visitors to an Egyptian mummy exhibit at the Anniston Museum of Natural History in Alabama in which they took an interpretive sign of 150 words and split it into three smaller signs. When there was a single sign of 150 words presenting information about the mummy cases on display, 12 percent of the visitors to the area stopped and read at least part of the sign. When that sign was replaced by three smaller signs, the number of people stopping and reading some of the text increased to 28 percent. The researchers concluded that the number of words contained in each sign influences the attracting and holding power of that sign.

Many other researchers have also recommended that the number of words on signs be limited (Bitgood, Finlay, and Woehr 1987; Serrell 1996a). Serrell (1996a) describes renovations to dioramas in the Field Museum of Natural History in Chicago, where new signs were limited to a maximum of fifty words. This was complemented by a short introductory panel of twenty-five words, which replaced the seventy-five-word panel that many visitors had generally ignored. Follow-up evaluation indicated that visitors moved more slowly through this hall than the other renovated sections, and that they also accessed more of the exhibit elements. The study also revealed that more visitors grasped the exhibit's main message, leading the researchers to conclude that reducing information had increased visitors' reading and understanding of the exhibit.

Although virtually all researchers and designers agree that "less is more," there is substantial variation in what is regarded as the optimal number of words per sign. The summary of recommendations in Table 4.3 illustrates that suggestions range from 50 to 150 words.

Table 4.3 Recommended Numbers of Words for Interpretive Signs

Recommended interpretive sign length	Source
40–90 words	Borun and Miller (1980)
50–75 words	Punt (1989)
150 words	Cross (1998)

One of the reasons for such variation may be that there is no simple and direct relationship between the number of words in a piece of text and the reader's perception of its length. For instance, Borun and Miller (1980) conducted a study in which they increased the length of a sign accompanying a display in a science museum and observed visitors' reading behavior. As the number of lines of text increased, the number of visitors stopping to look at the sign decreased dramatically (see Figure 4.5).

However, it must be noted that in this study, as the number of lines increased, so too did the number of topics. This is a common tendency in interpretive signs—often more words signify more topics. In other words, it may be the expected number of topics rather than simply the number of words that gives readers the impression that text is long. The lesson here is simple—limit the number of topics to two or three per sign and only include relevant information (Blakely 1981; Borun and Miller 1980; Punt 1989; Serrell 1996a). Above all, keep in mind that most interpretive signs are read while visitors are standing and that visitors may already have been walking around your site for several hours (Spencer 2002). This is physically tiring—long pieces of complicated text that require time and effort to digest are unlikely to appeal to those with tired feet!

Divide and Conquer

Another way to encourage visitors to read signs is to break up the text using headings, short paragraphs or chunks of information, and illustrations. Figure 4.7 presents four different versions of a sign designed to warn visitors to tropical rain forests about stinging trees often found along edges of paths and clearings. Version A presents the text as a page from a traditional textbook. Version B takes the same text and breaks it into shorter paragraphs or chunks. Version C keeps the

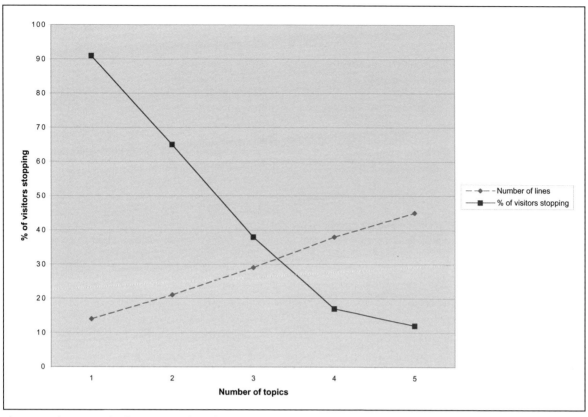

Figure 4.5. The connection between number of topics and time spent (Adapted from tables reported in Borun and Miller 1980)

Figure 4.6. Too much text can be very tiring.

traditional textbook format but uses direct conversational style. Version D both uses the direct, conversational style and breaks the text into smaller chunks or paragraphs.

These mock signs were shown to five groups of people. Four groups saw one sign each and were asked a series of questions about their recall of the main message and the information contained in the text. They were also asked to comment on the sign overall. The fifth group saw all four signs and were asked which they preferred and why. Table 4.4 (page 47) presents the results.

The study found that although readers preferred the text to be both broken up into smaller chunks and written in a conversational style, breaking up the text was the best improvement. Eighty percent of readers who gave their highest preference scores to the formats with broken-up text stated that they chose this format because they preferred text to be broken up into smaller pieces or

A

Although the serrated, heart-shaped leaves and fleshy red berries of the stinging tree often remind people of a raspberry bush, don't be tempted. Stay well clear!

Found primarily in the rain forest, the stinging tree has a dense covering of fine glasslike hairs on all exposed parts of the plant. If accidentally brushed against, the hairs break off and lodge in the skin. These hairs release a chemical that can cause a throbbing pain that can last many months.

Historical records show that animals are equally susceptible to the virulent poison produced by the hollow hairs of the stinging tree. Early settlers tell of horses being driven to self-destruction as a result of coming into contact with the plant.

C

As you walk through the rain forest, watch for a bush known as the Stinging Tree. This plant looks similar to a raspberry bush, with its heart-shaped leaves and fleshy red berries.
Don't be fooled! This bush bites!

The innocent-looking Stinging Tree hides a painful weapon. Look closely and you will notice the bush has a dense covering of fine glasslike hairs. If you touch a Stinging Tree, these fine hairs will lodge in your skin and the poison will cause an intense throbbing pain that can last for months!

Even horses have been driven to self-destruction by the pain caused by touching a Stinging Tree. So watch out for the Stinging Tree and if you see one, stay well clear!

B

The Stinging Tree is dangerous

The serrated, heart-shaped leaves and fleshy red berries of the Stinging Tree often remind people of a raspberry bush.

The Stinging Tree is not a raspberry bush.

The Stinging Tree has a dense covering of fine glasslike hairs on all exposed parts of the plant.

If accidentally brushed against, the hairs break off and lodge in the skin. These hairs release a chemical that can cause a throbbing pain that can last many months.

Historical records show that animals are equally susceptible to the virulent poison produced by the hollow hairs of the stinging tree. Early settlers tell of horses being driven to self-destruction as a result of coming into contact with the plant.

The Stinging Tree is found primarily in the rain forest.

Stay well clear!

D

Watch out—this bush bites!

This innocent-looking bush may look like a raspberry, with its heart-shaped leaves and fleshy red berries.

Don't be fooled!

The innocent plant looks like a dangerous weapon— the fine glasslike hairs that contain a nasty poison.

If you touch a Stinging Tree, these fine hairs will lodge in your skin and the poison will cause an intense throbbing pain that can last for months.

Even horses have been driven to self-destruction by the pain caused by touching a Stinging Tree.

Watch for Stinging Trees as you walk through the rain forest. If you see one, stay well clear!

Figure 4.7. Which one would you choose to warn people about stinging trees?

chunks. Readers criticized the two signs in the traditional page of text format for being too wordy or long, even though both signs had fewer words than one of the versions in which the text was broken into chunks. This suggests that breaking up the text also gives the illusion of fewer words.

This study is consistent with several others that have found that using headings and subheadings to break information into chunks improves a sign's visual appeal and makes it look less like a textbook (Dean 1994). This practice has also been linked with improved comprehension and recall of information (Cross 1998; Hartley and Trueman 1983; Kool 1985; Serrell 1996a;

Slivovsky 2001). Again, there is no universally accepted guideline regarding the optimum number of words per "chunk." Knudson et al. (1995) suggest paragraphs of no more than sixty words, and Dean (1994) suggests a limit of seventy-five words.

Another way to break up the text on a sign is to add illustrations (Aldridge 1993). The selection of appropriate illustrations and placement within the sign are discussed in more detail in chapter six; however, some examples are included here to demonstrate ways in which illustrations can be used to break up blocks of text.

Variety Is the Spice of Life

One of the basic principles of attracting and holding human attention is to avoid repetition. A common point of agreement among those researching interpretive design and reading behavior is that variety holds visitors' attention. Variety in signage refers to aspects such as font size, typefaces, and sentence and

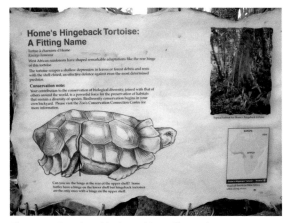

Figure 4.8. Imagine this sign with no illustrations.

paragraph length (Aldridge 1993; Cross 1998; Serrell 1996a). Varying these creates interest and can be used to clarify interpretive messages (e.g., different typefaces can be used to delineate different topics or points of view).

Variety is also important within sets of signs. Organizations often decide on a signature "look" for their signs and use this at all their attractions. Although this provides

Table 4.4 Readers' Perceptions of Different Sign Formats and Styles

Measure	(1) Traditional page of text Narrative style	(2) Text broken Narrative style	(3) Page of text Conversational style	(4) Text broken Conversational style
Readers able to list main theme	45%	63%	50%	68%
Readers saying this was the preferred format	2%	33%	3%	62%
Readers saying this was the easiest to read	1%	28%	4%	67%
Readers stating they liked the text broken up	——	79%	——	73%
Readers stating sign was too wordy or too long	40%	——	26%	——
Number of words	116	123	119	97

Source: Woods (1997).

continuity, there is a very real risk that visitors won't read the content because they assume it will be similar to messages previously encountered (Lackey and Ham 2003). Visitors need to be jolted out of this mind-set by varying elements such as

- the length of titles and the length of sentences (Serrell 1996a);
- the amount of text (Serrell 1996a; Zehr, Gross, and Zimmerman 1991);
- the use of humor, questions, and ambiguous statements in titles (Serrell 1996a);
- the use of examples or pieces of information to illustrate themes (Moscardo 1999); and
- the range of activities suggested to visitors (Moscardo 1999).

Having said that variety can be a good thing, it is important to remember the saying "All good things in moderation." This is especially true for changing typeface and font size too often. Using too many differences in the design features, such as different typefaces, color schemes, and formats, can be counterproductive because too much variety overpowers interpretive messages (Brochu 2003; Ham 1992; Trapp et al. 1994; Zehr et al. 1991).

Figure 4.9. Too much variety can be confusing.

Creating Visual Harmony

Visual harmony or balance is created by optimizing the use of white space and carefully positioning elements within the sign itself. White space is the area around the margins of text, between sections of text, and between text and illustrations. Because white space provides contrast and serves as a resting point for visitors' eyes, it is important to treat it as a tangible design element rather than simply the "leftover" piece (Parker 1997). You can use white space to emphasize particular elements of the sign, to divide text, and to signal relationships between text and illustrations (Denton 1992). In general, there should be more rather than less white space around the edges of a sign to keep it from looking crowded. White space between the components of a sign, such as paragraphs or illustrations, should be just enough to make it clear that the components are separate. Figure 4.10 provides some examples.

Apart from white space, other elements of an interpretive sign include illustrations, titles, and portions of text. Each element has its own visual weight. On the whole, the larger the illustration or piece of text, the greater its visual weight (Zehr et al. 1991). However, this visual weight also varies depending on the color of the text or illustration. For example, areas with color or contrast have a greater weight than black-and-white or monochromatic areas. In addition, areas with darker colors have a greater visual weight than those with lighter colors (Denton 1992). The visual weight of illustrations and text is also affected by their position on the sign—those toward the edge of a sign have more visual weight than those in the center.

A well-designed sign has elements positioned so that they create an even balance of visual weight. Ham (1992) likens this process to a seesaw in that sign elements must be positioned to ensure that the seesaw

Not enough white space—too crowded

White space is the area left around the margins of text, between sections of text, and between text and illustrations. In general you should leave more rather than less white space around the edges of a sign so that it doesn't look too crowded.

White space between the components of a sign, such as paragraphs and/or illustrations, should be just enough to make it clear that the components are separate.

Too much white space in the middle

White space is the area left around the margins of text, between sections of text, and betweem text and illustrations. In general you should leave more rather than less white space around the edges of a sign so that it doesn't look too crowded.

White space between the components of a sign, such as paragraphs and/or illustrations, should be just enough to make it clear that the components are separate.

Optimum amount of white space

White space is the area left around the margins of text, between sections of text, and between text and illustrations. In general you should leave more rather than less white space around the edges of a sign so that it doesn't look too crowded.

White space between the components of a sign, such as paragraphs and/or illustrations, should be just enough to make it clear that the components are separate.

Figure 4.10. White space—too much, too little, and just right

remains level. Although visual symmetry is desirable, Trapp et al. (1994) warn against dividing signs into squares or combinations of squares, claiming this arrangement lacks visual appeal. Rather, these authors suggest dividing signs into thirds. Regardless of the shapes chosen, however, the final result must appear balanced. Thus, if you place a large illustration on one side of a sign, you need to balance it with a large body of text on the other or a smaller piece of text and another smaller illustration.

Balance can be either formal or informal. Formal balance has perfect symmetry with an exact match between the elements on either side of the sign, and implies harmony, precision, and stability. Informal balance, on the other hand, relies on asymmetry. It is less strict and has a more dynamic "feel" (Trapp et al. 1994). To create informal balance, you can juxtapose text, illustrations, and white space on almost any axis. This approach is more flexible than formal balance because there are more possible points of attraction. It also has a more modern "feel" (Denton 1992). The style of balance selected should take into account the topic of the interpretation and the mood that you wish to convey.

Figure 4.11. Everything in balance and moderation

Color: The Good, the Bad, and the Ugly

Color adds variety, helps break up the text, and assists in conveying the theme of your interpretation. Color also introduces emphasis, contrast, and depth into interpretive signs. As a design tool, color can be used to attract attention, create moods, arouse emotions, and add visual interest to your signs (Parker 1997). In other words, subtle variations in color provide visitors with visual cues about the content and context of your exhibits and signs (Shaw 2002b). Most colors are associated with particular moods or emotions, and if carefully selected, can help to reinforce the interpretive message. Warm colors (reds, yellows, oranges) grab visitors' attention and can be used to highlight aspects of your sign. Because the wavelengths of warm colors are longer than cooler colors, they appear nearer, larger, and

more visible than cool colors (Denton 1992). In effect, warm colors are stimulating and give the illusion that the sign is advancing toward your reader. Thus, as previously mentioned, signs in bright bold colors such as red and yellow signal that the topic and associated materials are likely to be adventurous, fun, and interactive. Cool colors (blues, greens, violets) have shorter wavelengths and, as a result, make things look farther away. Physiologically, cool colors have also been found to slow down blood circulation, and are therefore regarded as more relaxing than warm colors (Denton 1992; Falk and Dierking 2000). Accordingly, cool colors are generally associated with quiet, more reflective activities.

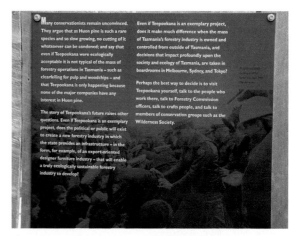

Figure 4.12. Color plays to your emotions.

In addition to setting the tone for interpretive material, colors can be used to signal particular topics—green is often associated with nature, spring, and peace; red signals aggression, warning, love, and passion; blue is commonly linked to oceans, heaven, serenity, and winter; and black is often associated with death, evil, and elegance (Denton 1992). Because the human brain compares visual input with learned models of the environment, color is a particularly effective way of representing environmental features. For instance, a bright ceiling can be used to represent daytime skies, whereas a dark one gives the impression of nighttime; warm colors are often used to represent sunlight or fire, whereas cold blue light can be used to create the illusion of moonlight or clouds (Shaw 2002a). You can also use color to delineate particular sign elements, such as headings, introductory paragraphs, key points, and take-home messages. This approach helps to highlight particular aspects of the sign, create consistency, and add visual interest (Parker 1997). Whatever the topic, it is important to choose colors that complement and support your theme(s), messages, and sign surroundings.

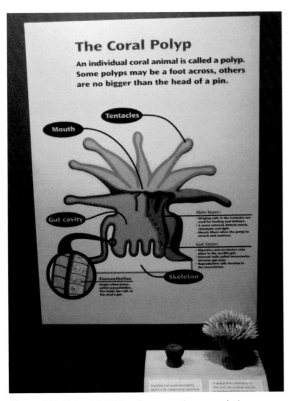

Figure 4.13. Color highlights for more than your hair

The following three attributes are commonly cited as reasons for incorporating colored elements into interpretive signs:

1. Color attracts and holds visitor attention.
2. Clear, strong contrasts between colors attract attention and enhance the legibility of text.

3. Dark-colored letters on a light background are particularly legible. However, when the text is part of a backlit slide or a sign in a shaded area, the reverse is true.

(Bacon and Hallett 1981; Borun and Miller 1980; Knudson et al. 1995; Serrell 1996a; Trapp et al. 1994; Wolf and Smith 1993)

Although some color combinations are visually appealing and work well together, others do not. Analogous colors are two or more colors that are consecutive on a color wheel. These create a unified "feel" and work well together due to their similarity. Colors directly opposite each other on a color wheel, known as complementary colors, also look good together. These combinations can be used to add emphasis, create excitement, and enhance a sign's visual appeal (Parker 1997). Don't be too adventurous, though, as overuse of color can create so much contrast that your readers may become confused and decide not to read any of your sign at all.

The recommended color combinations for text are blue, green, and black on white, beige, or cream. People find it least tiring to read black on white (Denton 1992). Although black on yellow and orange on white are also highly visible, they may not be appropriate for all settings. In ecotourism settings green and brown are popular choices. For example, the Queensland Parks and Wildlife Service in Australia uses brown on beige, and dark green on light green, cream, or brownish apricot for their signs.

When selecting colors for signage you should also consider color vision impairment. It is estimated that approximately 8 percent of the male population and 1 percent of the female population have some form of color impairment (Olson and Brewer 1997). This means that for every 100 visitors (fifty female and fifty male), eight men and one woman could be expected to have difficulty with some color combinations. The majority

For most interpretive signs it is better to use a dark-colored type on a light-colored background, as in the examples below.	You should only use light text on a dark background if the text will be part of a backlit slide in a dark place.
Blue text on a white or cream background is one of the options recommended.	Don't use red on green, as some people won't be able to read it.
Black on yellow is very easy to read but may not suit all places.	The red on green above also has a poor contrast. (for color vision impaired readers who can't read the box above)

Figure 4.14. Be careful when you mix colors.

of these color vision impairments will be red/green, but a small percentage will also have difficulty with yellow/blue combinations. As people with these vision impairments cannot distinguish between red and green or yellow and blue, avoid the following combinations: red on green or green on red, and blue on yellow or yellow on blue (see Figure 4.14).

Action, Action, We Want Action!

It is both possible and desirable to add interactive or participatory components to interpretive signs and exhibits. Interactive elements allow visitors to explore, manipulate, experiment, and generally follow their own interests for as much or as little time as they wish (Caulton 1998). Interactive components on signs and in exhibits can include three-dimensional models, features that visitors can touch or manipulate, and sliding or hinged panels that move to reveal more information. Although research examining the relationship between interactive elements and learning is in its infancy, it is clear that visitors enjoy participating in interactive activities, that interactive elements generate positive visitor attitudes, and that memories of such experiences are long-term (Caulton 1998; Falk, Scott, Dierking, Rennie, and Jones 2004; Spock 2004). Indeed, it is an oft-cited maxim in interpretation circles that visitors retain 10 percent of what they hear, 30 percent of what they read, 50 percent of what they see, and 90 percent of what they do (Hooper-Greenhill 1994).

Successful interactive signs and exhibits should have variable, open-ended outcomes and should be challenging but not threatening. You can invite visitors to examine, lift, listen, feel, turn, smell, taste, construct, jump, search, push, stroke, throw, draw—the range of interactive experiences is limited only by your imagination! Whatever the topic, your interactive signs and exhibits should be designed to develop skills, knowledge, and understanding, and should clearly state the actions required from visitors. Examples include "Look for the … "; "Pick up the ax and feel how heavy it is"; "Put your hand in the pool and feel how warm the water is"; "Stand at Position A and try to lift the block. Now stand at Position B and try again. What is the difference?" This approach entices visitors to participate by encouraging them to believe that participation will be enjoyable and beneficial (Caulton 1998). However, it is equally important that visitors be rewarded for their effort. Serrell (1996a) warns against asking simple questions such as "Do you know? …" and then offering a few more facts under a movable flap or cover.

As Tilden (1977) suggests, we should be asking provocative questions that arouse curiosity and encourage visitors to think carefully about possible answers. Serrell (1996a) also highlights the dangers of asking questions that the visitor cannot hope to answer before uncovering the hidden response. Instead, she recommends questions that encourage visitors to look at the rest of the sign, display, or setting to discover the answer. There must be an intrinsic reward for looking—the discovery should reveal useful, interesting, and meaningful information that will enrich the visitor experience. Challenge them to search for answers; to hear, smell, and touch; to solve riddles and puzzles; to make comparisons; and to come to decisions based on their activities (Veverka 2001). In sum, encourage visitors to think, to be mindful, and to learn!

A few words of caution, however: not all topics and materials lend themselves to interactive visitor experiences. Indeed, Caulton (1998) states that if the entire interpretation is reduced to hands-on activities, interpretive messages may become superficial and distorted. For instance, he warns against overusing the message that "science is fun," as it belies the fact that much of science research is slow and tedious. Hands-on interpretation may also be problematic when dealing with

topics such as convict brutality, war, the history of medicine, and other areas of human hardship and deprivation. So before you rush into designing interactive signs and exhibits, make sure there are a clear purpose and sound educational reasons behind their use, as well as an obvious connection between the interactive elements and your interpretive material. Another issue you need to consider is that if you invite visitors to touch, lift, or handle objects, they must be robust enough to withstand reasonably rough treatment. Materials such as silk and paper deteriorate rapidly and are not very suitable for interactive exhibits—for these objects you may need to provide replicas with similar properties (Knudson et al. 2003). We discuss the use of replicas further in chapter seven.

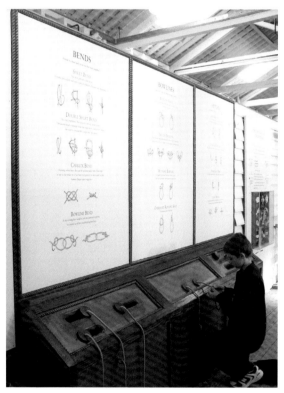

Figure 4.15. Signs, exhibits, and visitors interacting

Key Points

Visitors are more likely to read a sign if they believe it will be easy to read and that they will be rewarded with interesting and relevant information. You can encourage further reading by

- Writing in legible type that is big enough to see
- Using typefaces that are common and easy to read
- Having lines between forty and sixty-five characters long
- Having even spaces between the words and the lines
- NOT USING ALL CAPITALS
- Not using italics except in *short phrases for emphasis*
- Not splitting paragraphs across columns
- Writing in short rather than long paragraphs
- Covering one or two major topics
- Breaking up the text into short paragraphs with headings and subheadings
- Using illustrations
- Providing a variety of examples and suggested activities
- Varying sentence lengths and changing typefaces (but not too often)
- Using the right proportions of white space around and between the sign elements
- Balancing sign elements
- Using dark text on a light background in well-lit places and light text on a dark background in poorly lit areas
- Using strong color contrasts (except red with green and yellow with blue)
- Including interactive components

Chapter 5

Clear as Crystal:
Writing Text That Visitors Understand

In chapters three and four we discussed the features of signs and exhibits that attract and hold visitors' attention. However, these attributes alone do not guarantee that visitors will understand your messages or content. Signs must also be written in a format that is easy to understand and that facilitates learning.

The Power of the Written Word

The words we use on interpretive signs can summon up associations; shape visitors' perceptions; indicate the value of objects, places, and events; create powerful images; describe real events; and evoke emotional responses (Hooper-Greenhill 1994). Text can be written "from scratch" or can be taken from oral histories of those who have lived through particular experiences, from formal documents, or from poems, stories, or diaries. Words can be written in the speech patterns of those telling the story or can be "translated" into commonly used terms. Regardless of the approach taken, try to use words that visitors are capable of decoding or understanding—ones that clearly transmit the messages you intend.

Research has shown that there are a number of text features that make signs easier for visitors to understand. These include

- matching the text's level of difficulty with the audience's reading abilities,
- using simpler and shorter sentences, and
- avoiding jargon.

Figure 5.1 presents some examples of how not to write text for interpretive signs. Read through each sign and identify any aspects you think may cause difficulties for potential visitors.

Did you notice that the first two examples make a number of assumptions about what readers already know? All three examples use technical jargon and unfamiliar words that are likely to confuse readers. This is compounded by the use of long sentences with multiple phrases and modifiers. Another problem is that none of the signs has a theme, and in some cases the topic isn't even clear! Thus, although these signs may have titles, surroundings, and positioning that attract visitors and encourage them to read the text, it is unlikely they would understand what they are reading unless they are experts in the field. Writing text that is beyond the grasp of typical visitors is a dangerous trap into which many interpreters fall. Indeed, many museums and science centers employ experts in the field (e.g., geologists, physicists, etc.) to write their signs. Although the content may be technically correct, the ability of these experts to write in a manner that connects with visitors is highly variable. Accordingly, the remainder of this chapter is devoted to discussing methods of making signs easier to understand by integrating research on text design, literacy, and visitor comprehension.

KISS: Keep It Simple, Stupid

Tests of adult literacy suggest that text should be designed for an audience with limited

Some of the most radical and influential movements of 20th Century art can be identified with the Russian avant-garde—the experimental artists who invented and developed ideas such as Rayonnism (Mikhail Larionov and Natalia Gontcharova), Suprematism (Kasimir Malevich, Ivan Kluinkov, Kliun, Ivan Puni) and Constructivism (Vladimir Tatlin, Lazar (EL) Lissitzky, Alexander Rodchenko, Liubov Popova, Alexandra Exter, Naum Gabo).

Perhaps the most astonishing characteristic of the Russian avant-garde is the swiftness with which its representatives absorbed and developed styles such as French Cubism and Italian Futurism, combining them with indigenous cultural traditions and arriving at unique pictorial conclusions. For example, the dramatic shift from figurative to non-figurative art occurred almost overnight—with Tatlin's creation of his first abstract relief early in 1914 and with the public showing of Malevich's famous Black Square at the exhibition "0.10" in Petrograd in 1915.

(Chambers 1984, 49)

Arachnida

Almost all terrestrial with a few in fresh water. The prosoma carries a pair of chelicerae, a pair of pedipalps which may be sensory, grasping or otherwise modified, and four pairs of walking legs. The opisthosoma generally lacks appendages except for the spinnerets of spiders and the pectines of scorpions.

(Pierssene 1999, 57)

The scope of this paper has been purposely limited to woody species common to the bear/oak type as it seemed desirable to lay particular emphasis upon the winter season when woody species were not only heavily utilized in general as browse, but were even the sole food of deer following heavy snows.

(Heintzman 1988, 22)

Figure 5.1. We need to make sure the reader can follow us wherever we go.

literacy skills and that it should be as easy to understand as possible. Although visitors are eager to learn, they will be reluctant to spend too much effort and time deciphering exactly what it is that your signs are trying to communicate (Serrell 1996a). Consequently, to reach a wide target audience your signs should be easy to read and contain expressions that are generally well understood. According to Kool (1985), readability (how easy it is to read a piece of text) consists of three dimensions. The first is how easy the text is to read in terms of its physical features, such as line length, typeface, and size. The second is how interesting the material is to the reader. The third is how easily the words and sentences can be comprehended by the reader. It is this third dimension that we consider in this section.

There are many different systems to measure the readability of text. All require some counting of the number of words per sentence and the number of syllables per word. Using these and other similar measures, a score is computed, which is often given as a reading age. For a critical review of many of these readability tests the reader is directed to Woods et al. (1998). The formula and procedures for two commonly suggested tests, the Flesch Ease of Reading test and the FOG test, are presented in Table 5.1.

Table 5.2 illustrates how these readability tests can be used to assess a piece of text from an interpretive sign.

Although the results in Table 5.2 are what we might expect (i.e., the first piece of text is easier to read than the second), the two sets of scores highlight some of the problems with using these readability formulas (Klare 1974; Sawyer 1991; Serrell 1996a; Woods et al. 1998). First, "number of years of schooling" is not very precise. In some countries, sixteen years of education means some college education, whereas in others it does not. Even those with a college degree may still have no idea what the second piece of text means, because not only are the words long, they are also specific names for objects. In other words, a person needs a very special form of education to comprehend the content.

Second, different readability measures can give very different scores for the same piece of text. Woods and her colleagues (1998) took the text from twenty interpretive signs, analyzed it according to four different readability tests, and found little consistency in the outcomes. One sign, for example, was rated as difficult by one measure, could be read by a sixteen-year-old according to another test, and had a reading grade of seven or ten according to two other tests. This variation may be partly due to the fact that some words in English with a high number of syllables are not particularly difficult to understand (e.g., *caterpillar, vegetable*). As a consequence, tests relying on counting syllables to ascertain difficulty may be undermined by sign topic.

Third, many readability measures do not suggest what reading age is appropriate for a general audience. What reading age should we expect visitors to have? Authors of interpretation texts suggest target reading ages ranging from a minimum of a fifth-grade level (Knudson et al. 1995; Zehr et al. 1991) to a maximum of an eighth-grade level (Serrell 1996a) or a ninth-grade level (Sorsby and Horne 1980). Some of these recommendations are based on readability analyses of popular newspapers. According to Knudson et al. (1995), most newspapers are written at a fifth- to eighth-grade level,

Table 5.1 Two Readability Formulas

Flesch Ease of Reading test

1. Count the total number of sentences and words in the text.
2. Count the number of syllables in the text.
3. Calculate the average sentence length in words (the number of words divided by the number of sentences).
4. Calculate the number of syllables per 100 words (the number of syllables divided by the number of words multiplied by 100).
5. Calculate the reading ease score with the following formula.
6. Ease of reading = 206.835 − (0.846 times the number of syllables per 100 words) − (1.015 times average sentence length).

91–100 is Very Easy	51–60 is Fairly Difficult
81–90 is Easy	31–50 is Difficult
71–80 is Fairly Easy	0–30 is Very Difficult
61–70 is Standard	

Sources: Adapted for interpretive sign text by Woods et al. (1998, 61), and interpretation of scores from Trapp et al. (1994, 103).

FOG test

1. Find the average number of words per sentence.
2. Find the percentage of words with three or more syllables (not counting endings such as -ing, -ed, -es).
3. Add the results of steps one and two together and multiply this total by 0.4.
4. The result is the number of years of schooling needed to understand the material.

Source: Kool (1985, 33).

Table 5.2 Two Readability Formulas Applied to the Same Piece of Text

Interpretive text

The innocent-looking stinging tree hides a painful weapon. Look closely and you will notice that the bush has a dense covering of fine glasslike hairs. If you touch a stinging tree, these fine hairs will lodge in your skin and the poison will cause an intense throbbing pain that can last for months.

Flesch Ease of Reading test	FOG test
54 words, 3 sentences 69 syllables Average sentence length = 18 Number of syllables per 100 words = 128 206.835 – (0.846 times 128) – (1.015 times 18) = 80.277 The Flesch Ease of Reading test suggests this text is fairly easy to read.	Average number of words per sentence = 18 Percentage of words with three or more syllables = 1/54 times 100 = 1.85 (only one word has more than three syllables according to the rules) (18 + 1.85) times 0.4 = 7.94 The FOG test suggests that you would need to have eight years of education to understand this material.

Interpretive text

Almost all are terrestrial with a few in freshwater. The prosoma carries a pair of chelicerae; a pair of pedipalps that may be sensory, grasping, or otherwise modified; and four pairs of walking legs. The opisthosoma generally lacks appendages except for the spinnerets of spiders and the pectines of scorpions.

Flesch Ease of Reading test	FOG test
50 words, 3 sentences 87 syllables Average sentence length = 16.7 Number of syllables per 100 words = 174 206.835 – (0.846 times 174) – (1.015 times 16.7) = 42.68	Average number of words per sentence = 16.7 Percentage of words with three or more syllables = 12/50 times 100 = 24 (16.7 + 24) times 0.4 = 16.28 The FOG test suggests that you would need to have at least sixteen years of education (i.e., a bachelor's degree) to understand this material.

whereas Sorsby and Horne (1980) found that British newspapers ranged from a seventh- to ninth-grade level. An important assumption that these authors make is that the majority of adults have no difficulty reading these newspapers. However, international studies of literacy suggest that many adults worldwide do in fact have difficulty reading newspapers (Australian Bureau of Statistics 1997 and 1998; Organisation for Economic Co-operation and Development 2002). Table 5.3 lists the literacy levels for twelve countries and regions and what the different levels mean.

Note that typically people at one level cannot do the tasks described for the next level. Thus, 17 percent of Australians and 21 percent of Americans from fifteen to seventy-four years old cannot usually complete the tasks described in level 2, namely, use a flyer to find out where to get more information about a topic, locate information about a new law in a fire safety article, identify which movies are comedies in a set of short movie reviews, or use information in an article to explain what happens when a plant is exposed to low temperatures (ABS 1998; OECD 2002). The literacy research also found that although greater levels of literacy were generally associated with more education, 56 percent of people with bachelor's degrees

Table 5.3 International Adult Literacy Levels

Country or Region	Level 1 %	Level 2 %	Level 3 %	Level 4 %
Australia	17	27	37	19
Belgium	18	28	39	14
Canada	17	26	35	23
Germany	14	34	38	13
Ireland	23	30	34	13
Netherlands	11	30	44	15
New Zealand	18	27	35	19
Poland	49	35	20	3
Sweden	8	20	40	32
Switzerland (French)	18	34	39	10
Switzerland (German)	19	36	36	9
United Kingdom	22	30	31	17
United States	21	26	32	21

Level 1
    Can locate information on a medicine label giving the maximum number of days medicine should be taken
    Can locate and underline a sentence in a newspaper article describing what a swimmer ate
    Can locate one piece of information in a short fire safety article

Level 2
    Can use information in an article to explain what happens when a plant is exposed to low temperatures
    Can use a flyer from a personnel department to find where to get more information
    Can locate information in a fire safety article about a suggested new law
    Can identify which movies are comedies in a set of short movie reviews

Level 3
    Can determine, from text only, which movie review is the least favorable
    Can list three situations for which a doctor can be consulted from information on a medicine label
    Can explain how to check for correct bicycle seat height according to a page in a maintenance manual

Level 4/5
    Can extract three pieces of information from a pamphlet
    Can in own words describe one difference between two types of job interviews outlined in a pamphlet
    Can list two examples from a lengthy newspaper article that illustrate the main argument of the article

Sources: ABS (1997, 1998); OECD (2002).

and 46 percent of people with postgraduate qualifications had literacy levels of 3 or lower.

These problems have led some researchers to advocate the use of comprehensibility tests as an alternative to readability tests. Comprehensibility tests differ from readability tests in that they require a sample of the audience to actually read the text and then complete a test to assess how much they have understood.

These tests are recommended because they provide a clear assessment of how easy or difficult a target audience will find the text (Kool 1985). The procedure for conducting a cloze test for comprehensibility is described in Table 5.4.

Woods et al. (1998) compared the readability tests described earlier with the cloze comprehensibility test and found that overall, none of the readability tests correlated well with the comprehensibility test.

Table 5.4 The Cloze Test for Reader Comprehension of Text

The cloze test procedure

Take a piece of text and delete every fifth word (or closest to fifth if the fifth is an article or conjunction such as *a, and, the*, etc.).

Ask a sample of readers to fill in the missing words.

Calculate the average percentage of correct answers across the sample.

> 60% correctly completed on average is Independent level (a person will not require assistance to attain a high level of understanding from the text).

40–60% correctly completed on average is Instructional level (a person will understand the text if provided with some instructional assistance such as illustrations).

< 40% correctly completed on average is Frustration level (a person is unable to read the text effectively).

Example of a cloze test (full text available in Table 5.2)

The innocent-looking stinging _____ hides a painful weapon. _____ closely and you will _____ that the bush has a _____ covering of fine glasslike _____. If you touch a _____ tree, these fine hairs _____ lodge in your skin and the _____ will cause an intense _____ pain that can last _____ months.

Examples of alternatives for deleted words (underlined)

If a dinosaur were <u>seen</u> today, it would be sensational. (alternatives—*here, alive*)

From giant trees to small <u>species</u> on the forest floor (alternative—*plants*)

In general they have less of everything <u>typically</u> found in tropical rain forests. (alternatives—*usually, that is*)

These conifers are important <u>representatives</u> in deciphering fossil records. (alternatives—*tools, assets, sources*)

Some plants have special features that <u>allow</u> them to survive on the forest floor. (alternative—*help*)

Source: Woods et al. (1998, 52, 56).

They concluded that comprehensibility tests were a better option, not only because they gave a clearer indication of how much difficulty actual readers would have, but also because these tests provided specific ideas on how to improve the text. For example, the second part of Table 5.4 provides some of the words readers used to fill in the gaps—these could be used as alternatives to make the text easier to understand.

The conclusion for interpreters is that the simpler the text in a sign, the better. Based on literacy data, it seems wise to target text at the fifth-grade reading level and to help the reader to understand the key points using as many different aids as possible. However, for variety you can add the occasional word that is more complex and colorful. Provided your sentences still make sense, even if these more complex words are not clearly understood, readers with less ability will still gain meaning from reading your sign (Serrell 1996a).

Getting the Message Across: Selecting Effective Text

One of the simplest ways to ensure that your sign is clearly expressed is to read it out loud. Is the combination of words rhythmic and easy to say, or do you tend to trip up on

Table 5.5 Examples of Rules to Make Text Simpler and Easier to Read

Rule	What to avoid	What to replace it with
Keep sentences short.	A number of… At the present time … Due to the fact that … For the purpose of … In the near future … The month of June … Make preparations for … Make use of … Indicative of … In the case of … In addition to … At one time … Would seem to indicate …	Some Now Because For, to Soon June Prepare Use Shows If Besides Once Means
Simplify sentences by limiting the number of qualifying phrases.	The bluebird has, as a result of unequal competition for nest holes with starlings, among other causes, declined in numbers. Of all the insects that teem on the surface of our Earth, including those that buzz in our ears, eat our crops, infest our homes, and generally make our lives miserable, flies are the worst. The foredunes, with their irregular topography, are in an area of natural instability where sometimes the dune-building processes are in ascendancy, whereas at others, the forces tending to break down the dune prevail.	Bluebirds have declined in numbers for many reasons. But the main reason is competition with starlings for nest holes. Of all the insects that teem on the surface of our Earth, flies are the worst. The foredunes are irregular because the area is unstable. Some dunes are being built up by sand deposits, and others are being eroded.
Use shorter, more familiar words.	Assistance Has the capability Consequently Endeavor Equitable Expedite Indicate Magnitude Methodology Preclude Terminate Utilize Nevertheless Notwithstanding Pendant	Help Can So Try Fair Hurry, speed up Show Size Method, way Prevent End Use Still In spite of Hanging
Get to the point.	The formation of Azure Island is mainly attributed to northerly longshore ocean currents that bring sand from southern states with southeasterly winds moving the sand particles up the beach. It is generally accepted that the continental shelf is the main source of sand in the creation of these islands.	Most of the sand on the beaches of Azure Island comes from the continental shelf. Sand particles are brought here by ocean currents from the southern states and are moved up onto the beach by southeasterly winds.
Express statements in the positive.	The exhibit won't be ready until Monday. The burrows will not collapse provided people don't walk on the dunes. These nocturnal animals will come out of their burrows if visitors are quiet.	The exhibit will be ready on Monday. The burrows will collapse if people walk on the dunes. These nocturnal animals only come out of their burrows once visitors stop talking.
Use verbs rather than nouns or adjectives from verbs.	We experienced an increase in visitor numbers last month. Our intention is … I make a recommendation that … The harvest required the involvement of every person in the community. Land clearing has led to a reduction in the number of koalas living in this region. Our prediction is that …	The number of visitors increased last month. We intend … I recommend that … The harvest involved every person in the community. Land clearing has reduced the number of koalas living in this region. We predict that …

Sources: Derived from Knudson et al. (1995, 214–16) and Heintzman (1988, 15, 17, 22–23).

certain words? If it's difficult to say, chances are your visitors will also find it difficult to read. Readability research suggests the following practices make text easier to read:

- Keep sentences short, generally no more than fifteen words.
- Simplify sentences by limiting the number of qualifying phrases.
- Use shorter, familiar words and avoid jargon and technical terms.
- Get directly to the point by writing in concise sentences and ensuring that the lead sentence is important. Signs and exhibits should pack a punch rather than ramble on with wordy explanations.
- Express statements in the positive rather than the negative. Say what something is, rather than what it is not.
- Use verbs (action words) rather than nouns or adjectives derived from verbs.

(Adapted from Dean 1994; Heintzman 1988; Knudson et al. 1995; Punt 1989; Serrell 1996a; and Zehr et al. 1991.)

Table 5.5 provides examples for each of these rules, as well as some alternatives that can be used in interpretive text.

Selecting the words and expressions you intend to use is only part of the process—you also need to make sure these are combined in clear, grammatically correct sentences. Signs that are grammatically incorrect or contain spelling errors are unprofessional and have little credibility (Beck and Cable 2002). In fact, visitors may infer that the information is also incorrect and start to question the basis of your whole interpretive program. The checking procedure should also involve looking for words and expressions that could have a double meaning. Are the words clear and unambiguous, or is it possible that some

visitors will interpret your text in a way you never intended? Words have strong personal and cultural connotations, so you need to be careful that your signs are not vague, confusing, or offensive. Even an everyday word such as *cow* may conjure up a range of associations—milk, gentle, T-bone steak, manure, and sacred, just to name a few. The implication is obvious—check and double-check your signs with readers from a variety of backgrounds to ensure that what you've written will be processed as intended.

Up Close and Personal

One of the simplest ways to engage your visitor is to treat the interpretation as a conversation between you and your visitor. Humans tend to use active sentence structure naturally when we speak to each other—all the more reason why you should read your text out loud. Good interpretive signs draw visitors in by presenting information as though it were part of a conversation. The best way to create this conversational style is to write with active, vivid verbs and use pronouns such as *you, me, I,* and *we* (Cross 1998; Ham 1992; Heintzman 1988; McManus 1989; Rand 1985; Rudin 1980; Slivovsky 2001; Volkert 1991; Zehr et al. 1991). We have demonstrated the merits of using an active style in Figure 5.2—note that the sentences in the "active" column tend to create more vivid images than their "passive" counterparts.

The stinging tree example described earlier in this chapter also illustrates how to change from a traditional passive, nonpersonal style to a more direct, active, personal style through the use of both active language and personal pronouns. The original text was replaced by a sign that links the information directly to the reader and uses the pronouns *you* and *your.*

Figure 5.2 Passive or active—which sounds better to you?

Passive	Active
Orientation signs are read by most visitors.	Most visitors read orientation signs.
High standards of waste management have been implemented by this resort.	We have implemented high standards of waste management.
These seedlings have been devoured by grasshoppers.	Grasshoppers have devoured these seedlings.
The way Grandma starched our shirts is something I'll never forget.	I'll never forget the way Grandma starched our shirts.
Birds, possums, and small snakes impose a heavy toll on cicada populations.	Cicada populations are destroyed by birds, possums, and small snakes.
The northerly movement of sand is due to longshore drifts.	Longshore drifts move sand in a northerly direction.
Before entering, visitors are asked to remove their shoes.	Please remove your shoes before entering.

ORIGINAL TEXT

Found primarily in the rain forest, the stinging tree has a dense covering of fine glasslike hairs on all exposed parts of the plant. If accidentally brushed against, the hairs break off and lodge in the skin. These hairs release a chemical that can cause a throbbing pain that can last many months.

REVISED TEXT

The innocent-looking stinging tree hides a painful weapon. Look closely and you will notice that the bush has a dense covering of fine glasslike hairs. If you touch a stinging tree, these fine hairs will lodge in your skin and the poison will cause an intense throbbing pain that can last for months.

Another example is presented below.

ORIGINAL TEXT

The site chosen by mosquitoes to lay eggs must contain water for the duration of the aquatic stages. If the female detects potential predators such as fish in the water, she is unlikely to choose this site. Avoid leaving potential breeding sites such as buckets and plant trays, which fill up with water.

REVISED TEXT

Mosquito eggs must be laid in water; however, female mosquitoes will not lay eggs where there are potential predators. You can deter mosquitoes by stocking ponds with native fish and emptying out any potential breeding sites such as buckets and plant trays.

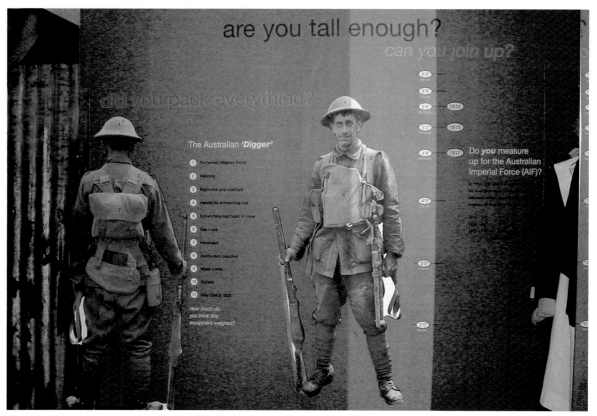

Figure 5.3. Getting personal can be a good idea.

Making Important Connections

A core principle of effective interpretation is that the theme and content must connect with the visitor. The best themes are those that build a personal connection between the topic and visitors' experiences. These connections can be to their everyday lives, previous experiences, or their immediate on-site experience. The stinging trees example in the previous section turns a description of an interesting rain forest plant into a more personal threat to the visitor. The text is much more closely focused on the theme "Beware of these trees; they will hurt you."

You can connect with your visitors by

- Finding human characters related to the topic and telling their story
- Creating links between the site, topic, and/or event and visitors' home environments and daily lives

- Defining the implications of the processes and/or activities described in the interpretation for visitors' everyday experiences, and vice versa

Stories are powerful interpretive techniques because they get your visitors emotionally involved and provide personal insights into the topics being discussed (Regnier et al. 1994). Storytelling gives life to a subject, injecting it with color and excitement. Regardless of the topic or audience, good stories should follow a logical sequence and be written in such a way that visitors can hardly wait to read what happens next (Pierssene 1999). According to Strauss (1995, 27): "[The story] is the heart and soul of every effective slide show, film, puppet show, living history or costumed character presentation."

Effective stories use expressive language that clearly conveys the emotions and

William Day married his first wife, Elizabeth, on 1 July 1828. We know this because he was tattooed with her initials and the date of their marriage. He later deserted Elizabeth and married another woman called Ann Thompson. His tattoo may have given him away because Day was transported for bigamy. While at Port Arthur, Day was employed as a porter in the Commissariat Store. Like other convicts who worked in trusted positions, Day was rewarded for his efforts with small payments of tea and sugar. He was not charged with an offence during his time at Port Arthur.

To find out how different life would have been for William Day had he been sent to work in the gangs, walk through the door marked 'Demotion.'

Figure 5.4. Everyone loves a good story.

experiences of the central characters. They often use an intimate and conversational tone, and include humor, slang, quotes, anecdotes, and dialogue (Blake and Hamilton 1995). These techniques all serve to give the story a poignancy and immediacy that cannot otherwise be achieved (Hooper-Greenhill 1994), as illustrated in Figure 5.5.

Stories can also be used to convey information about nonhuman topics. For example, the life cycle of plants and animals can be explained by giving them human qualities and describing the world through their eyes. Thus, you could interpret hermit crabs by telling the life story of Harry the Hermit Crab and his seemingly never-ending search for a bigger home; you could compare cuckoos' use of other birds' nests to dropping children off at day care; you could interpret trees by explaining how they germinate and grow. An example is presented in Figure 5.6—note how the story version makes the topic come to life.

Inanimate objects can also be interpreted using this technique. For example: The old wreck *settled comfortably* back on the ocean floor and *waited patiently* for the next group of curious visitors to arrive (Blake and Hamilton 1995). This approach is particularly effective with children (Ballantyne et al. 2000).

As mentioned, another way to build personal connections is to directly relate interpretive content to what visitors are experiencing while reading your sign. Tilden (1977, 13–14) provides a simple example in his reporting of the following interpretive text accompanying a museum display in

Housework on the Frontier

Peggy lived in this tiny hut with her husband and seven children. Housework was very difficult for pioneer women—dust and dirt seemed to get everywhere!

Each day Peggy would sprinkle wet tea leaves on the wooden floors to dampen down the dust before sweeping out the hut. Once a week she would hand-wash all the family's dirty clothes and sheets in this big wooden tub and drape them over the shrubs outside to dry.

So next time you do housework, think how lucky you are to have washing machines, dryers, and vacuum cleaners to help!

Figure 5.5. Another good story

Fig Tree Facts

Age: About 500 years

Height: Nearly 50 meters

Trunk Circumference: About 39 meters

Fruits: Fleshy black or purple fruits produced during the wet season

---

Turning facts into a story

A strangler fig starts life high in the forest canopy where a seed is dropped by a bird or bat into the fork of a tree. The seed germinates and the fig may live on high as an epiphyte for many years.

When conditions are right, the fig sends fine cablelike roots down the host's trunk to the ground. These roots act as feeding tubes and the plant grows rapidly.

The roots fuse to encircle the host tree. By restricting the sap flow to the canopy the strangler fig may eventually kill its host.

Figure 5.6. Lists of facts versus a story

Texas: "'Prehistoric mammoths were here in Texas just a few thousand years ago. They roamed the plains in great herds … The chances are that they browsed right where you are standing now.' Where you are standing now. With that statement the mammoths are not far away creatures of time or space but right under your feet."

The sign in Figure 5.7 uses this principle of directing visitors to look, listen, or think about where they are. Slivovsky (2001, 3) offers some more examples of how to directly involve the visitor with the following list:

- See the stripes on this bird?
- Look for lemurs doing—.
- Ever build a bird house?
- How would you feel if—?

This approach works best if visitors can view the object under discussion from where they read the sign, although with wildlife this is impossible to guarantee. In such cases, you may need to accompany the text with a photograph. If you do decide to pose questions to create connections, try to select ones that visitors themselves would probably ask,

such as "Why don't the sharks eat the fish living with them in the tank?" or "Why is this called art?" (Serrell 1996a, 106). The best way to choose relevant questions is either to listen to visitors while they are viewing interpretive material or to directly

Figure 5.7. Stop, look, listen, and think.

ask them what it is that they are interested in. As we mentioned earlier, questions should only be included if they can be answered by reading your signs or by examining the immediate interpretive setting.

Key Points

Visitors will only read your signs if they are written in a language that is easy to understand. Although the Flesch Ease of Reading test and the FOG test have been used to evaluate the readability of visitor signs, both have inherent problems. These problems can be overcome by using the cloze test for reader comprehension, which has the added advantage of eliciting visitors' suggestions for alternative words that would make the sign easier to read.

Practices that improve the readability of text include the following:

- Writing in short sentences (no more than fifteen words)
- Limiting the number of qualifying phrases

- Using short, familiar words and avoiding jargon
- Writing in a concise format
- Writing in the positive rather than the negative
- Using verbs rather than nouns or adjectives derived from verbs

Adopting a conversational style (i.e., using first and second person and active verbs) also improves readability, as does the practice of relating a sign's content to what visitors are experiencing here and now. Some common techniques to achieve this include the following:

- Finding human stories related to the topic
- Creating links between the site, topic, and/or event and visitors' home environments and daily lives
- Defining the implications of the processes and/or activities described in the interpretation for visitors' everyday experiences, and vice versa
- Telling stories that follow a life theme

Chapter 6

Lighting the Spark:
Techniques to Foster Visitor Learning

In the previous chapter we emphasized the importance of writing in clear, concise language that encourages visitors to read and understand your signs. Several other techniques that improve the appeal of signs and the clarity of messages include

- connecting to visitors' prior experiences,
- developing "word pictures" using analogies and metaphors,
- using themes,
- presenting information in layers, and
- using illustrations.

In this chapter we present methods and recommendations for using these techniques, as well as examples and photographs to illustrate how they improve sign clarity.

The "Aha" Moment: Lifelong and Free Choice Learning

Much of what we know about the world in general is learned from informal sources such as television, newspapers, the Internet, museums, and libraries (Falk and Dierking 2002). Informal or "free choice" learning environments such as museums, parks, and zoos usually have broader aims than formal learning settings and are designed to appeal to a wide range of audiences. Thus, many free choice learning experiences are (or should be!) designed to encourage curiosity and exploration; reinforce or challenge attitudes; help visitors to develop a sense of

personal, cultural, and community identity; and encourage visitors to make decisions about moral and ethical issues (Falk and Dierking 2000; Hein and Alexander 1998; Schauble, Leinhardt, and Martin 1997; Uzzell 1998).

Much current research in free choice learning environments focuses on how visitors make sense of the information they encounter (Ballantyne and Packer 2005). Falk and Dierking's (2000) Contextual Model of Learning is widely used to investigate and understand free choice learning. This model assumes that learning is constructed over time, and that it is the product of interactions among three overlapping contexts—the personal, the sociocultural, and the physical (see Falk and Dierking 2000 for an in-depth discussion of this theory). The model recognizes that people have a range of prior experiences and motivations for learning and that these influence the way humans experience the learning environment. In other words, learning is a cumulative process that draws from a wide variety of sources over long periods of time.

What implications does this have for designers of free choice learning sites such as parks, museums, science centers, zoos, and historical sites? Basically, it means that when designing interpretive signs and exhibits, you need to link your information to the prior knowledge, experiences, interests, and motives of your key visitor groups. In other words, you need to relate new information to something your visitors already know. To illustrate the importance of this process, we

69

need to examine how humans process and store information.

People learn by connecting pieces of information and then fitting new information to what they already know. According to Schiffman (2001), the process of assimilating new information into memory occurs in three main stages, as illustrated in Figure 6.1.

The first stage is the **sensory store**, in which information that comes through our senses is filtered for processing. To explain how this works, let's follow Arthur, Martha, and Junior through the Diamantina Dinosaur Park. Imagine there are two replica dinosaurs and a large interpretive sign framing the entrance. The sign focuses on the evolution of different dinosaur species. Junior is completely mesmerized by the replicas—he sees the sign but it doesn't catch his attention and is instantly forgotten. Meanwhile, something about the sign attracts his parents' attention (perhaps one of the elements we discussed in chapter three—extreme, bright, colorful, moving, unexpected, or ambiguous things, and/or messages, images, and stories that have personal relevance).

Arthur and Martha both read the sign, and the information enters their second stage of memory, the **short-term store**. Information can be held here for only a few minutes. Unless they actively process it at this stage, it

will be forgotten. There are two ways they can process the information. They can repeat it, which is how many of us remember passwords, telephone numbers, and PINs. Alternatively, they can connect the pieces of new information to each other and to things they already know—sort of like doing a jigsaw puzzle. Arthur has been fascinated by dinosaurs since he was a young boy and has a wealth of knowledge about different species. He easily links the information to displays he remembers from childhood visits to the local museum. Messages on the interpretive sign slot neatly into his mental framework or schemata and become stored in his **long-term memory**. Martha, on the other hand, has no interest in dinosaurs and only came to the park to "keep her boys happy." She knows very little about dinosaurs and struggles to make sense of the information presented—"What's all this Triassic, Jurassic, and Crustaceous stuff, and what's the difference between theropods, sauropods, and stegosaurs?" In the end she finds it too difficult to decipher and simply walks away. For her, the interpretive messages did not connect together in any meaningful way, nor did they connect with anything in her existing schemata. The result? Very little of the interpretive message made it into Martha's long-term memory. In other words,

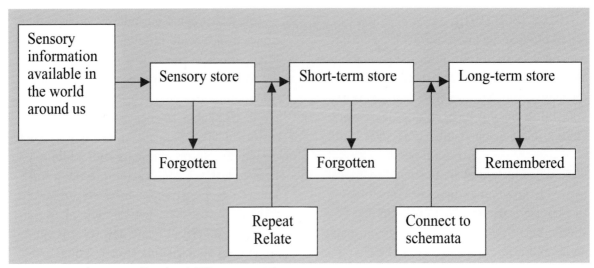

Figure 6.1. Stages in memory (Based on Schiffman 2001, 192)

it is unlikely she learned much from reading the sign.

The lesson for interpreters is obvious—you need a current, reliable indication of your main visitor groups and their knowledge, motives, experiences, and interests *prior* to designing your interpretive signs and exhibits. This information can be obtained from commercial tourism statistics as well as in-house surveys (see chapter nine for methods of designing and conducting front-end, formative, and summative evaluation). If your site attracts mainly Marthas, introductory signs should provide visitors with sufficient background knowledge to understand the topics being discussed. Be aware, however, that it is not necessary or desirable to keep repeating the same "introductory" messages over and over because visitors' schemata will change and develop as they assimilate new information.

To illustrate this concept, when one of the author's sons was first learning to talk, he used the word *dog* to refer to dogs, horses, cats, geese, bicycles, horses, and lawn mowers. The word *dog* for him was the label for a simple schema that roughly meant "things that moved and were found in a backyard." These objects all shared the features of moving and being found in the backyard. He began this schema by direct experience with the family's two dogs. His parents gave him the label *dog*, and he applied it to everything he found that moved and was in a yard.

With increasing experience he began to change this schema. So, for example, he found that dogs, geese, and horses shared the extra characteristics of accepting food from him. Bicycles, mowers, and cats, however, weren't interested. So he had to split his simple schema into two schemata. One for things that moved in backyards and ate his food and one for things that moved in backyards and wouldn't eat his food (these all became bikes for a while). With increasing

experience he developed more schemata that became more complex. So now as a teenager, he not only has separate schemata for each of these things, but his schema for *dog* is substantially more complex. It now includes information about a variety of different breeds, about how to react to different types of dog behavior, and, after a recent seminar on pet care by a local vet, a detailed section on dog parasites.

These examples demonstrate that the better you are at designing signs that place objects, features, and events into a meaningful context, the greater the chance of your visitors assimilating the new information (Falk and Dierking 1992). Effective interpretive practice not only helps visitors to understand the topic, but also allows them to personalize the information. For instance, a sign that describes wash day in the life of nineteenth-century women is likely to be more effective if it is accompanied by a replica nineteenth-century kitchen with the original washing implements. Your sign could describe the items and how they were used; the items themselves enable visitors to imagine how they were used; and your kitchen exhibit puts the whole interpretation into context. This approach is likely to trigger personal reactions and mental leaps such as "Hey, I remember my great-grandma had one of these in her closet. That's what it was for!"

Interpretive topics, however, are not always that straightforward—sometimes we may need to interpret information that is controversial, unfamiliar, or not widely practiced or accepted by society. If visitors don't have the necessary schemata, how can we present information in a meaningful way? Because humans are very good at changing, adjusting, and selecting new information so that it matches what is already known (think of three-year-old children!), we need to design experiences that minimize the chances of visitors manipulating or rejecting new information (Baron and Byrne 1997;

Moscardo 1999). The best way to do this is to work from the familiar to the unfamiliar, or the known to the unknown, as this helps visitors understand and accept your interpretive messages. If you don't do this, visitors will find it difficult to understand your messages and will be unable (and possibly unwilling) to connect the new information to their existing schemata.

You can help visitors build a bridge between new information and their existing schemata by

- connecting new information to things visitors already know using examples, analogies, and metaphors; and
- making very clear connections between pieces of information. It is much easier to assimilate a list or series of points if the items are linked or classified in some way—this is why the use of themes is so critical.

We discuss these strategies in more detail in the following sections.

Bridging the Gap: Using Analogies and Metaphors

Analogies and metaphors enable visitors to create links between their previous experiences and your interpretive message(s). They are particularly useful in helping visitors take the step from the familiar to the unfamiliar, the known to the unknown. Because analogies emphasize the similarities between something familiar and something new, it is important to use common objects and experiences that provide visitors with visual images and reference points.

Some more examples of analogies are presented in Figure 6.3—note that the new information is related to something that almost all visitors would be familiar with.

Metaphors, on the other hand, describe objects using words that are generally used to

Figure 6.2. Connecting to what people already know

describe something very different (Ham 1992). These figures of speech add color and interest to interpretive text and are an important method of attracting and maintaining visitor attention as well as helping visitors assimilate the new information into their existing schemata. Some examples are presented in Figure 6.4.

Connecting the Dots: Themes Again!

As mentioned, a strong theme that links interpretive material together and captures the attention and interest of visitors is an integral part of interpretive planning. A good, clear theme can also be an important aid to visitor understanding, as it helps visitors connect pieces of information together. A small number of published studies have been conducted on visitor preferences for topics and ways of organizing information. Washburne and Wagar (1972) asked visitors to identify the exhibit they found most

In the same way as humans huddle round log fires in winter, lizards lie in the sun to warm up.

The avocado tree acts as nature's fridge because the fruit only ripens once it's picked.

If you have kids, you'll know just how quickly they grow out of their clothes. Hermit crabs are the same—they regularly outgrow their shells and have to find new and bigger ones.

Like balloons, the seeds of this plant float to wherever the breeze takes them.

A rainforest is a bit like an apartment block—each "level" has different décor and residents.

Coastal plants are the sand dune's overcoat—they prevent waves from washing away the sand, and protect the dune from rain and wind.

This tree can grow to the height of a ten-story building and produce enough fruit in one year to make 200 jars of jam.

Figure 6.3. Using analogies

interesting in four centers in national parks and state forests in the Pacific Northwest. The researchers examined the characteristics of popular exhibits and found that visitors preferred information presented as cause-and-effect relationships or connected in some way, such as through a story. The visitors in this study did not like information presented as isolated facts. Prince (1982) repeated this study with visitors to two centers in North York Moors National Park in the United Kingdom. Results were similar—visitors preferred information to be connected together in some way rather than presented as a list of facts. Likewise, Walker (1988) reported on visitor opinions of exhibits designed for the Royal Ontario Museum in Canada. Again, visitors preferred the pieces of information to be organized as a story or by a theme of some kind.

The tanks stormed onto the battlefield.

The waves pounded the shoreline, greedily devouring the exposed sand dunes.

Deceit erodes the foundation of human relationships.

Chocolate—the comfort blanket of children and adults alike!

About ten minutes after sunset, an eerie quiet descends on the reef. The coral passages are silent, deserted, and vaguely menacing. This quiet period lasts only about 15 to 20 minutes. The director shouts "action," the nocturnal animals burst onto the set, and the scene changes to night maneuvers.

Figure 6.4. Making metaphors

Cicadas

- Female cicadas lay approximately 200–300 eggs in batches of 20 in slits they make in the bark of a tree.

- Eggs hatch into nymphs.

- Nymphs fall to the ground and search for cracks to burrow into. They dig down to 40 cm–1 m and make a cell underground.

- Nymphs seek food from roots that protrude into their cell.

- Nymphal development can take from 9 months to 17 years, depending on the species. In this time they shed their skins about four times.

- Nymphs emerge when conditions are suitable—usually on warm nights in early summer.

- Adult cicadas live 2–4 weeks, during which time they mate frequently. The females lay eggs and the whole cycle starts again.

Figure 6.5. Cicadas—just the facts

Cicadas—Masters of Underground Living!

A cicada starts life as an egg laid in a slit in tree bark. When the egg hatches, the cicada (called a nymph) drops to the ground and looks for a crack to burrow into. It digs a burrow approximately 40 cm to 1 m long and makes itself an underground home right next to the tree roots. The nymph feeds on the sap in the tree roots, and stays buried in its underground home for between 9 months and 17 years (depending on the species). During this time the nymph grows and sheds its skin about four times.

Cicadas finally emerge as adults on a warm night in early summer. They live above the ground for only 2–4 weeks. During this time they mate frequently, the females lay eggs, and the whole process starts again.

Figure 6.6. Cicadas—the whole story

From a learning perspective, developing themes to link together pieces of information makes intuitive sense, as this process helps visitors to see the connection between their current knowledge and the facts, figures, and stories presented. Although we as interpreters may think the relationship between pieces of information or topics is obvious, visitors often lack our specialist knowledge and are therefore unable to make the same cognitive links. Indeed, interpreters often become so involved and familiar with their own specialized areas that they forget that for visitors, much of the information is new and completely unfamiliar (think back to Martha at the dinosaur park).

Figures 6.5 and 6.6 demonstrate how using a theme "glues together" pieces of new information and presents a seamless interpretive story. Note how the new information is linked to common experiences and how the sign tries to create a bridge between the familiar and the unfamiliar.

Each to Their Own: Layering Text

Layering or organizing information into a hierarchy is a very effective way to help visitors understand your message and choose how much detail they want to read. It is unrealistic to expect visitors to read *every-thing* on interpretive signs. Indeed, research shows that visitors are very selective in what they read, and that their choice is generally based on what they find visually appealing, interesting, or personally relevant (Falk and Dierking 1992; McManus 1994). As we mentioned in chapter three, selective behavior becomes more apparent the longer the visitor is in the interpretive setting. Initially, visitors tend to read and interact with almost all signs and exhibits, but as the visit progresses, the number of signs that capture their attention decreases. It is a rare visitor who reads every single word on every single interpretive sign! Rather, observational studies suggest that all visitors read some signs, but no visitor reads all. According to Falk and Dierking (1992), this is not surprising, given that it would take an adult several days to read every sign in a medium-sized museum.

So how can we ensure that the majority of our visitors read and process messages we consider important or even crucial? As mentioned in chapter three, one way is to position important information where it is easy to see and access. In other words, signs should be positioned in visitors' direct line of vision and/or at major decision points or entrances. Another way to highlight important messages is to divide interpretive signs into "layers." Layering or organizing information into a hierarchy not only makes information easy to see, but also allows visitors to choose what they read and to pursue the topics in which they are most interested.

Ham (1992) suggests organizing interpretive text in signs and displays into four parts or levels:

- Level 1 includes the title and a short introduction to the theme.
- Level 2 refers to the subheadings that divide the pieces of text.
- Level 3 is the main body of the text and

key illustrations. In this section the information can be divided into several layers:

> - The first layer is intended for all readers and contains the main example or point of the theme.
> - The second and third layers provide more detailed information or examples for those who want to pursue the theme further.

- Level 4 includes ideas about what visitors can do with the new information. This could consist of one or two suggestions for activities visitors can do at the site or things they can do after their visit.

Figure 6.7. Using layers to organize information

Each layer is distinguished in some way, such as the size of the text, the use of sub-headings, or physically presenting the information in a hierarchy from top to bottom. The aim is to arrange the information so that visitors only have to read the top

The Koala

Koalas sleep for 18 hours a day. The rest of the time is spent eating. They eat 1.5 kg of leaves every day—that's about three bucketfuls! Koalas feed on only 12 species of the 100 species of eucalyptus trees. They have very long intestines to help them digest tough leaves. Please be careful approaching these animals, as they may scratch if you frighten them.

SSHHH! I'M LIKELY TO BE ASLEEP!

Koalas sleep for 18 hours a day. The rest of the time is spent eating.
They eat 1.5 kg of leaves every day—that's about three bucketfuls!

Koalas feed on only 12 species of the 100 species of eucalyptus trees.
They have very long intestines to help them digest tough leaves.

Please be careful—koalas may scratch if you frighten them.

Figure 6.8. Comparing different approaches to the same topic

layer of a sign to get the main message quickly and easily. If they are interested in a more detailed understanding of the material, they can read further.

Layering enables interpreters to clearly state the main interpretive, safety, or conservation messages and ensure that these messages don't get lost among all the others. Figure 6.8 illustrates two signs that contain exactly the same information. First read the top example and state what you think is the main message(s). Now read the second

BANDICOOTS

- Bandicoots are small, ratlike marsupials. (introduction)
- Bandicoot numbers are declining rapidly due to domestic and feral cats. (theme/layer 1)
- Bandicoots are largely nocturnal. (layer 2)
- Bandicoots eat insects and some plants. They have large claws that enable them to scratch for insects. (layer 2)
- The second and third toes of bandicoots' hind feet are fused together. (layer 3)
- Some bandicoots, such as the eastern barred bandicoot (*Perameles gunnii*) and the bilby (*Macrotis lagotis*), are very rare and are only found in limited areas. (layer 3)
- Cats are the greatest threat to the survival of bandicoots. (reiteration of theme and take-home message)

Figure 6.9. Lists of facts

BANDICOOTS

Bandicoots are small, ratlike marsupials whose numbers are declining rapidly.

Predators
The main predators of the bandicoot are domestic and feral cats.

Habits
Bandicoots are nocturnal, though can sometimes be seen during the day. They mainly feed on insects, and have large claws that enable them to dig up food. Bandicoots also eat some species of plants.

Other facts
Like the wombat and kangaroo, the second and third toes of bandicoots' hind feet are fused together. Some bandicoots, such as the eastern barred bandicoot (*Perameles gunnii*) and the bilby (*Macrotis lagotis*), are very rare and are only found in limited areas. Cats are the greatest threat to the survival of bandicoots.

The survival of many species of bandicoots is in our hands. If you have a cat, please put a bell on its collar!

Figure 6.10. Using layers to organize facts

example. Is it easier to define the main message in this format?

Serrell (1996a) describes the use of layering in signs and exhibits and makes the important point that interpreters sometimes confuse detail with difficulty. Successive layers should not become more difficult to read. Rather, each layer of information must still be written and organized according to the principles we have already outlined. That is, the extra layers provide extra information and detail, not extra complexity. An example of how to use layering when presenting information is given in Figures 6.9 and 6.10—note that the level of complexity remains the same throughout the sign.

Picture This: Designing Meaningful Illustrations

You can also make text easier to understand by including illustrations that relate to your sign's message(s). Images and illustrations are an integral aspect of sign design and, when combined with text, can be used to enhance, expand, compare, contrast, and highlight aspects of your interpretive message. Illustrations used on interpretive signs range from paintings, photographs, and sketches to scanned images, line art, clip art, graphs, diagrams, and maps. According to Carter (1997), the best use of illustrations is to show visitors what they can't actually see (e.g., inside a camera, a beaver's den, or a rocket ship) or to give them an idea of what

Figure 6.11. Using illustrations to help visitors "see" what isn't really there

a particular place or structure may have looked like in previous times (e.g., an abbey, medieval London, the pyramids).

In 1992 Falk, Philips, and Boxer reported on a study of visitors to an electricity and magnetism exhibition at the California Museum of Science and Industry in Los Angeles. The exhibit was made up of a series of interactive displays that aimed to provide visitors with an understanding of various concepts by encouraging them to conduct personal experiments through participating in the displays. As staff felt the exhibition was not meeting these objectives, a series of interpretive signs were added to the displays. These signs included a short question directing visitor attention to the concept and an illustration of how the display worked. Visitor responses were recorded both before and after the installation of the illustrated

signs. The researchers found that with the new interpretive signs the amount of time visitors spent in the exhibition increased by 50 percent, their use of the interactive displays doubled, and there was a significant and substantial increase in their conceptual understanding.

These results are consistent with other research in education and psychology, which has found that people find it easier to understand and remember text when it is accompanied by illustrations (Mayer and Gallini 1990; Williams 1993). Williams (1993) reports on a review of studies comparing learning from illustrated and nonillustrated text. In forty-five of the forty-six studies, readers learned more from the illustrated than from the nonillustrated text. On average, the illustrated version produced a 36 percent improvement in readers' understanding of the text. According to Williams (1993), this research shows that illustrations can be useful to

- Bring to life objects, people, or places mentioned in the text
- Explain abstract structures, such as food webs and ecosystems
- Show spatial relationships, such as the connection between different types of habitat and proximity to water
- Demonstrate procedures, such as how to operate an interactive display
- Provide a context for unfamiliar information, such as a drawing of how an ancient Roman site would have looked before it was abandoned
- Emphasize key points in the text in order to help visitors remember it

Too often illustrations are used simply to fill up space or to make signs "pretty." This rarely works well, as unnecessary illustrations tend to make signs look cluttered and can distract visitors from the main interpretive message, as is evident in Figure 6.12.

When planning interpretive signage it is important to develop the theme and text prior to selecting illustrations—remember, the illustrations are there to support the theme and messages, not the other way around. In other words, illustrations should serve to enhance and simplify aspects of the interpretive message. Unfortunately, many designers make the mistake of beginning with the illustrations they have and then try to fit a message or theme around these. As Ham (1997, 7) argues, "the design process must concern itself *first* with the message and the communication strategy of imparting this message to a particular audience, and then (and *only* then) with the important task of making it pretty, durable and visually appealing."

One way of ensuring that illustrations match and enhance your interpretive

Figure 6.12. Don't use illustrations just because you can.

messages is to develop interpretive plans that clearly state the purpose and content of supporting illustrations. An example of this approach is presented in the Eastern Lake Ontario case study.

Regardless of the type of illustration, there are some common rules suggested by various authors (e.g., Aldridge 1993; Ham 1992; Williams 1993).

- The illustration has to be relevant to the text. Illustrations should support text by helping visitors digest and understand it. To do this effectively, there must be a logical relationship between the two, with the illustration (be it a diagram, map, or photograph) clarifying and enhancing the text. Visitors' attention is automatically drawn to illustrations, and they will assume that there is a connection between them and the text. If the relationship between the two is unclear, the illustration will only create confusion.

Case Study: Eastern Lake Ontario Sand Dune and Wetland Area

When designing interpretive signage for the Eastern Lake Ontario Sand Dune and Wetland Area, interpreters carefully planned each step of the process. First, they developed a suitable theme that would underpin all interpretive signage in the area. Once this had been agreed on, text was written and fine-tuned. The theme and text were then used to develop a plan that outlined the purpose and nature of each illustration. This plan shows the connection between text and illustrations—note how the theme and text logically lead to the selection of appropriate illustrations.

Use of illustration	Text	Proposed illustrations
Represent abstract concepts	Sand dunes grow and change as windblown sand is trapped by plants. Wetlands become more lush as water levels change, and plants die and decay into the soil. Dunes and wetlands are also a rich storehouse of plants and wildlife, from shorebirds and cottonwood to egrets and duck weed.	Cross section of a high dune with wetlands behind
Show spatial relationships	Lake Ontario is so big you can't even see the other side! There are five great lakes of varying sizes and depths in North America: Superior, Michigan, Huron, Erie, and Ontario. Lake Ontario is the smallest, but not the shallowest (Lake Erie is). Lake Ontario has about a quarter of the surface area and half the depth of Lake Superior.	Map or satellite photo of Great Lakes region
Demonstrate procedures	Sand dunes are very fragile and easily eroded. Please stay on the designated trails and use dune walkovers.	Dune walkover
Provide a context for the unfamiliar	Do you think the soil under your feet is just dirt? Well, look again. There are all kinds of creatures, such as moles, earthworms, and ants, making it their home. Some of them, such as bacteria, are so small you can't see them with the naked eye.	Cross section of ground showing soil layers and decomposing log
Emphasize key points	A colony, or group, of bank swallows is living in the steep sides of these dunes and they don't like visitors! Bank swallows build their nests by digging or burrowing into the cliff. When disturbed they leave the nest, endangering their young.
Please don't walk in or disturb this area.	Bank swallows going into cliff nest

Source: Text and suggested illustrations taken from Earnest (1994, 6–11).

- Illustrations shouldn't be so complex that they need their own explanation. At best an illustration will not need any extra text at all. An exception would be a simple identification label or caption. Essentially, graphics should enable nonreaders or those with limited language skills (e.g., international visitors) to grasp the sign's main concepts.
- Illustrations should demonstrate one main idea. Just as with text, it is important not to overload visitors with too much visual information.
- Illustrations should use labels instead of legends and keys. Labels are easier to process than legends and keys because they require visitors to take one less cognitive step in order to understand the message.
- Illustrations should follow the same design principles as those that apply to text. Illustrations should be balanced and be surrounded by enough white space so that they don't seem crowded. Variety is also important, as using exactly the same size illustrations throughout the sign becomes visually boring. In addition, less is often more—a few larger illustrations have a

greater visual impact than many smaller ones. The last thing you want is for your interpretive message to be drowned in a sea of illustrations (refer back to Figure 6.12).

Key Points

Visitors learn new information by relating it to their prior experiences and knowledge. Interpretation works best when it takes visitors from the familiar to the unfamiliar, using interpretive techniques such as

- analogies,
- metaphors,
- examples, and
- themes.

Visitor comprehension is also enhanced by layering text to suit different levels of interest. This approach enables interpreters to place the predominant interpretive messages up front and ensures that important messages are accessed and understood by as many visitors as possible. Illustrations can also increase visitors' comprehension, provided they are carefully selected to support and clarify the themes and content of the interpretive signs.

Chapter 7

Meeting the Challenge:
Creative Techniques for Special Purposes

To this point we have discussed interpretive design issues in broad, generalized terms. However, some topics, sites, and groups of visitors may require special consideration, and it is to these we now turn. In this chapter we deal with some tough yet important issues—how to interpret controversial or emotive events, sites, and artifacts; how to design meaningful immersion experiences; how to select sites and interpretive content for trailside signs; how to interpret works of art; how to make exhibits and signs accessible to visitors with physical, sight, hearing, or learning disabilities; and how to design experiences that appeal to older adults.

"Hot Interpretation": Arousing Visitors' Emotions

In some interpretive settings, meaning is embedded in the site or within the objects on display. This is particularly evident in places that cater to visitors who have had direct experiences with the topic under discussion. Consider artifacts of war such as machinery and photographs—these generally evoke powerful images and memories for those who served in the war being depicted. Reliving these memories can be highly emotional, particularly if the topic itself is emotionally charged (e.g., conflict, poverty, violation of human rights). In such cases, the site or the artifacts themselves trigger stories and memories *within* the visitor therefore background information or interpretation can be minimal. If, however, the audience includes visitors who do not bring these memories or

personal stories with them, more detailed interpretation may be required to help them to make sense of the signs and exhibits. That is, visitors with no direct experience need relevant background facts and stories to make the topic come alive.

In the past, great care has been taken to present controversial and emotive issues (such as cultural heritage, environmental/industrial/racial/religious conflicts) from a factual or neutral perspective. Museums in particular have been very careful to avoid presenting controversial exhibits and signs that could divide or annoy their visitors (Cox 2002). Traditionally, war museums have interpreted the weapons or "toys" of war rather than the human impacts of conflict. Suffering was often presented in terms of courageous and heroic sacrifices, and the effects of conflict and injury on the permanently maimed or the families of those killed in battle were rarely mentioned. Recently, however, there has been a trend toward using a more emotive approach to interpreting such topics. Accordingly, complex issues such as war are being interpreted using diary extracts from those who experienced it or by focusing on the emotional upheaval created in the lives of those left behind (Pearce 1991). This approach highlights the personal impacts of war and helps visitors understand the fear, despair, friendship, joy, and anguish experienced by soldiers and their families. As an example, Shackley (2000) describes the In Flanders Field Museum in Belgium, where visitors receive an identity card of a soldier who was killed while fighting in the region.

Visitors insert the card into computers at different points in the museum to find out what happened to "their" soldier. In this way, the war is seen through the eyes of one individual, and the story is brought to life using the testimonials, poems, letters, and diaries of a real soldier. Exhibits are also accompanied by the noise of artillery and the smell of trenches to convey the awful conditions experienced.

Interpretation that confronts controversial issues is referred to as "hot" interpretation because it engages visitors' emotions and challenges their values

Case Study: Using Hot Interpretation to Present Information about Apartheid

District Six in Cape Town once housed a vibrant, mixed-race community; however, on February 11, 1966, it was declared a white area. During the following fifteen years, 60,000 people were forcibly removed, resettled in government-provided "apartments," and their houses razed to the ground by bulldozers. The District Six Museum is located in the deconsecrated Methodist Church, one of the few remaining buildings at the edge of the desolate, weed-choked rubble of what was once District Six. When the museum officially opened in 1994, ex-residents of the district were the priority visitor group, and the museum was committed to providing a rallying point for dispossessed people, a place where "people could express their anger and grief over this structural violence" (McEachern 1998).

Today the museum attracts an ever-increasing number of international visitors. These visitors come to the site with experiences and prior knowledge that differ markedly from those of the original clientele. With the change in focus of the District Six Museum from a place for ex-residents to reflect and express their feelings to one that interprets and celebrates the history and significance of the area, the place of emotion in the visitors' experience needs to be reconsidered. Interpretation at the museum is naturally "hot" for ex-residents and those with direct experience of the event because the artifacts tap into their memories and personal stories. However, these artifacts may not engender similar emotional responses in nonresidents because they do not bring similar experiences and memories to the museum environment.

Visitors' evaluations of the museum indicate that there is indeed a difference in the way local and international visitors perceive and experience it. Local visitors are satisfied with viewing artifacts, photographs, and mementos of the events surrounding the evacuations and do not request further interpretation of the events or apartheid. International visitors, on the other hand, admit they have limited knowledge or experience of forced evacuations and apartheid. Many express a lack of awareness of these events and an interest in learning more about what really happened. Although they find the artifacts interesting, this group seeks more information about the people who were actually involved and how apartheid affected their daily lives. In other words, international visitors want artifacts put into a familiar context to enable them to directly relate to the events described.

Visitor responses suggest that the museum needs to design scaffolded interpretation to help international visitors make connections between the concept of apartheid and their own previous experiences and knowledge. Recommendations include installing introductory panels at the entrance that explain apartheid and the events at District Six, a structured route through the displays, and personal stories that illustrate what the apartheid system meant to those living within it. It was also suggested that hot interpretive displays be designed with two main purposes—to challenge visitors to contemplate how they would react in similar situations, and to encourage them to reflect on evidence of injustice in their own attitudes, actions, and societies. In particular, it was recommended that visitors be encouraged to channel the emotions evoked by exhibits into actions that promote racial tolerance, justice, peace, and understanding in their own communities.

Dropping the atomic bombs

The dropping of the atomic bombs arguably the most significant event in history, remains controversial. Some condemn the Allied decision because the bombs killed thousands and inaugurated the atomic threat to humanity. Others argue that they actually saved lives. Japan's surrender prevented a costly Allied Invasion of Japan itself. It also saved many thousands of Allied prisoners of war who were weakened from years of captivity. many more prisoners would have been killed in massacres planned by the Japanese commanders.

The Sandakan–Ranau 'death march'

In late 1944, about 2,600 Australian and British prisoners were held at Sandakan in Borneo. They were starved, routinely beaten, and worked till they dropped, leaving them weak and sick.

In 1945 the Japanese feared a revolt by the prisoners as Allied forces approached Borneo. They sent groups fo the "fittest" prisoners on gruelling "death marches".

The prisoners walked through dense jungle to Renau, a village 260 kilometers away. All but six men died on the marches. Of the prisoners left behind in the camp at Sandakan—the weakest and sickest—not one man survived.

Figure 7.1. Hot interpretation

(Ballantyne and Uzzell 1993). It is specifically designed to provoke emotive responses, and goes beyond simply relaying neutral, "cold" facts. Using hot interpretation to explain an event or issue "attempts to ensure that visitors do not leave a site, or experience without being emotionally involved" and aims to "engage the public's attention and challenge them to examine their attitudes and actions with respect to specific social, environmental and moral issues" (Ballantyne and Uzzell 1993, 4–5). We argue that if museums and other interpretive sites are serious about their role in shaping visitors' learning and understanding, they should be willing to take on the responsibility of addressing issues that may provoke and/or disturb some visitors. Interpreters must be prepared to design signs and exhibits that confront rather than avoid emotive and controversial issues. By presenting different perspectives, you can

- encourage your visitors to question their own beliefs and values;

- promote their personal reflection; and
- enhance their understanding of other people's beliefs, attitudes, and viewpoints.

The Hot Interpretation Case Study presented on page 84 describes research conducted by Ballantyne (2003), which explores how hot interpretation could be used to interpret aspects of apartheid at the District Six Museum in South Africa.

Hot interpretation can also contribute to reconciliation, healing, and community development. To do this well, your signs and exhibits must be sensitive to the ideas and values of both visitors and the different interest groups and stakeholders. Wherever possible, your interpretive content should incorporate community views. Furthermore, you will need to negotiate the themes, stories, and facts with community groups prior to implementation, particularly if there are cultural restrictions on dissemination of information. Two examples of hot interpretive signs are presented in Figure 7.1—note how contentious issues have been confronted rather than glossed over.

Some places have substantial emotional meaning for visitors—your interpretation must allow for this. Many visitor sites have become associated with human suffering, and in such cases, it is important to ensure that the interpretation is not seen to trivialize the events or present them as entertainment (Shackley 2000). Although it is tempting to think that every event, site, or feature can be interpreted, there are cases where interpretive signs and exhibits may not be required or indeed desired by visitors. Pilgrimage sites, religious sites, and war memorials often fall into this category—visitors already know why they are special! If people are anticipating a place of quiet contemplation and reflection, the presence of interpretation of any kind may be viewed as intrusive (Carter 1997).

Get Down and Dirty: Creating Immersion Experiences

Immersion experiences envelop visitors in the sounds, smells, textures, and tastes of a place or event. Well-designed immersion experiences enable visitors to see and experience real things within meaningful contexts, and encourage them to become totally absorbed in the interpretive experience (Falk and Dierking 2000; Knudson et al. 1995). Generally, immersion experiences feature multisensory elements that give visitors the impression they are part of the feature, event, or place being interpreted (Lumney 1994).

Some common immersion techniques you can use to augment signs and enhance the perception of "reality" include the following:

- **Smells of the era or site**, such as baking bread for an exhibit on kitchen design through the ages, hay for a farming exhibit, or machinery for an exhibit on the Industrial Revolution.

Smell is very effective in triggering memories but is rarely used in interpretive sites (Mayrand 2002). One notable exception is the Jorvik Viking Centre in York, United Kingdom, where visitors "travel back" in time cars to experience a Viking village, complete with the smells of fish and middens.

- **Sounds** that create an ambiance, stir the imagination, and/or evoke memories. For example, the Museum and Art Gallery of the Northern Territory, Australia, has a small room where visitors can stand in the dark and hear the sound of vicious winds scraping against tin roofs, just as residents did during Cyclone Tracy, which tore the city of Darwin, Australia, apart on Christmas Eve in 1975. Sounds are also commonly used to evoke an era—popular music, television programs, radio programs, the sounds of horses and carriages on cobbled streets are all linked to particular historical periods; another example is the sounds of air raid sirens and low-flying aircraft, which are closely associated with World War II. You need to be careful, however, that the noise of these exhibits does not overpower or detract from nearby signs and exhibits.

- **Recorded stories** spoken in the dialect and words of a particular historical period.

- **Everyday items and artifacts** that are placed within the context in which they were used. Visitors tend to be very interested in the daily lives of others—how and where they washed, slept, ate, and so on. Exhibits and signs that can place these activities in context and demonstrate how they were conducted are always popular (Robertshaw 1997).

- **Audiovisual displays** and virtual reality exhibits that simulate situations visitors may not normally be able to experience. These can be applied to a wide range of topics, such as visiting an underground gold mine, flying through the Grand Canyon, trekking through the Himalayas, and being inside a termite mound. Virtual reality can also be used to simulate historic events, such as the Great Fire of London or the building of the pyramids.

Research at the Anniston Museum of Natural History in Alabama showed that features such as thematic backgrounds, signs, and creative use of films and graphics can transport visitors into another time and place (Bitgood, Ellingsen, and Patterson 1990, as cited by Knudson et al. 2003). By designing multisensory exhibits and effective interpretive signage, we can give visitors a fairly realistic impression of what it must have been like to be a monk in the Middle Ages, a factory worker in the Industrial Revolution, a Crusader in the Middle East, a cook in a nineteenth-century manor house, and so on. Some authors (e.g., Jordanova 1989; Sorensen 1989) have criticized immersion experiences for being highly selective and glossing over the less pleasant aspects of history. Although there is an element of truth in this, from the interpreter's point of view this selective interpretation is necessary, as some aspects of history are difficult for visitors to visualize or experience. Modern visitors have different knowledge, attitudes, and beliefs from their ancestors, and may be unable (or unwilling) to fully transport themselves back to a time when hardship, abject poverty, disease, and brutality were an accepted part of life. Subjecting visitors to immersion experiences, such as a session in a torture chamber or medieval medical procedures, is unlikely to foster positive word-of-mouth advertising or repeat visitation! Thus, although immersion experiences enable us to replicate aspects of other times

and locations, they do not enable us to provide total simulation (Robertshaw 1997). Nevertheless, with careful planning and attention to detail, immersion experiences can provide visitors with unparalleled insight into the topic, site, or event being interpreted. As with all interpretation, it is vital that research for immersion experiences and signs be meticulously conducted—the events, clothing, phrases, artifacts, buildings, and attitudes *must* reflect the attitudes and experiences of the time if they are to give visitors a sense of being transported to that era (Knudson et al. 1995).

Staying on Track: Designing Sets of Signs

In some situations, such as along trails or boardwalks, you may need several signs to adequately convey your interpretive message. When designing sets of signs, there needs to be a balance between contrast and harmony. If every sign in a set looks the same as the one before, they soon become monotonous and will no longer attract visitors' attention. If, however, you use a range of similar elements, your signs become linked by these common elements and a harmonious effect is created (Gunn 1994). As an example, you could keep the sign material, borders, and general layout the same, but use text, illustrations, and colors that clearly signify the content is different. Each sign should flow on logically from the one before, picking up the story line and enticing your visitors to move forward through the interpretive experience. Remember, though, that if visitors are likely to encounter most or all of your signs in one visit, sign messages should complement, not duplicate, one another (Ham and Weiler 2000).

As with all interpretive signs, the selection of a theme to link the content of several signs together is vital. Themes help to structure a trail or walk, and also help you choose what to interpret and where to position your interpretive panels. The following procedure for designing interpretive trails is adapted from the Department of Environment and Heritage (1998), Knudson et al. (1995, 2003), and Trapp et al. (1994):

1. Plan the route of the trail.
   • Define the theme, purpose, and objectives of the interpretive experience.
   • Select a trail that will provide variety and interest in the way of vegetation, views, features, and structures.
   • Walk the proposed trail, noting places and points of interest.
   • Select sites/features that will support the theme chosen (avoid those that are temporary, such as nests and plants that have a very short flowering season). Make sure it will be safe and convenient for people to stop there.
   • When choosing sites, consider whether your visitors are likely to see or hear something that needs interpreting, or whether they will miss seeing or hearing something if you don't point it out (Knudson et al. 2003).
   • Ensure that the sites/features selected will logically fit into a series of signs. The number of signs will vary depending on the length of the trail; however, a quarter-mile trail (approximately 400 meters) will generally accommodate about ten signs (Pilley 1990, as cited by Knudson et al. 2003).
   • Ensure that the proposed trail's distance and terrain are within the capabilities of the target audience. Interpretive trails are generally between one and two miles, and usually loop back to the starting point. A loop formation will enable you to use one point as both the entrance and exit, and has the added advantage of reducing the number of walkers your visitors are likely to encounter.
   • If possible, create clearings that allow scenic views and access to interesting vegetation. Design the trail so that it curves out of sight, as this will entice your visitors to continue walking.
   • Walk the trail in the morning and the afternoon to determine whether sunlight and shadows are likely to affect your signs' readability. Will visitors see your signs in the afternoon shadows? Will signs reflect the rising/setting sun and therefore be difficult to read? Will your signs have interactive elements that may be too hot to touch in the midday sun? Brochu (2003) describes a visitor attraction in Texas that erected metal Braille signs in full sun—if the designers had only thought this through prior to installation, they could have saved time, money, and a lot of burned fingers!

2. Write the interpretive text following the principles outlined in chapters three to six. Knudson et al. (2003) recommend using no more than fifty words per sign. If possible, incorporate multisensory experiences into the trail by asking visitors to search, touch, smell, and listen.

3. Design an introductory sign for the start of the trail that clearly outlines the theme of the walk, its length, and its degree of difficulty (Ham 1992). If possible, include an orientation map and highlight any points of interest (e.g., rock formations, waterfalls, old buildings, etc.).

4. Design sign mock-ups and place them in the proposed sites. Test these with site staff (and if possible, a representative

sample of visitors) to check whether the content is clear, the "story" or train of thought is logical, the theme is obvious, and the directions are clear. Revise content where necessary.

5. Finalize the sign design, ensuring you use some common elements (sign materials, borders, size, and font) to make it obvious that the signs are linked.

6. Install the interpretive signs according to the principles of "best practice" signage placement (see chapter three). Remember that a sign should never obscure the feature it interprets. If possible, place the first two signs close together to assure visitors they are going in the right direction, but avoid the temptation to clutter your trails with interpretive signs, as this is likely to ruin your visitors' sense of exploration and discovery (Hughes and Morrison-Saunders 2002).

7. Install seats if there are sites that have detailed interpretation, good vantage points, or features that visitors may wish to sit and observe.

If families and children form a large proportion of your target market, consider painting/etching directional signage on the footpaths to entice younger legs to complete the walk. These should fit the theme of the trail. For example, a rain forest trail could use fern leaves imprinted in the paving stones as a way to highlight the direction of the trail and encourage children to move along it. Regular rewards, such as answers to questions or hidden "treasure," could also be incorporated into the trail (for more discussion on this topic, see chapter eight).

Beauty Is in the Eye of the Beholder: Interpreting Art

Traditionally, art galleries have been designed on the premise that visitors derive meaning from simply viewing the art on display (Wright 1989). In other words, the art is expected to "speak for itself"; therefore the accompanying signage is limited to simply providing the name of the work, the artist, and the date it was created. This approach may be sufficient for those who are intimately familiar with the techniques, history, and development of the style of art being displayed because they can interpret it for themselves. It does little, however, to fuel the interest, knowledge, and enjoyment of the art novice. Indeed, those with limited art knowledge are often baffled by the works on display, fail to grasp their significance, and can often do little more than judge the works based on whether or not they have immediate visual appeal.

Noel COUNIHAN
born Australia 1913 died Australia 1986
travelled frequently from 1939

Boy in helmet
1968 Melbourne
screenprint on paper

National Gallery of Australia   1984.1572
A National Gallery of Australia Travelling Exhibition

Figure 7.2. Interpreting art is not as easy as you might think.

As interpreters of art, you need to ask some key questions about your visitors that will enable you to design signs and interpretive stories that will attract, interest, and inspire novices and experts alike. Wright (1989) suggests that prior to mounting an exhibition on paintings, curators need to consider what visitors know about

- the topics depicted in the paintings;
- the skills and techniques involved;
- the materials that were used and how they differ from what is available today; and
- the underlying scheme that enables art historians to categorize paintings into different genres, such as impressionism and cubism.

As with all interpretive sites, you need to build a bridge between the work of art and the everyday experience of your audience (Museums Australia 1998). Thus, to fully appreciate the works of art on display, you will need to give your visitors background information on the topics listed above, as well as insight into the social conditions, values, customs, and censorship processes of the time. Placing the work in the context of the artists' other artistic efforts (Staiff and Bushell 2003), and highlighting details such as features of the landscape, domestic decorations and clothing styles, will also help your visitors make connections between the painting and their own experiences and knowledge.

Information can be presented on interpretive signs and/or by surrounding the piece of art with relevant memorabilia from the period in which it was created. The latter technique was used to redevelop the Laing Art Gallery in Newcastle, United Kingdom, where each section in the "Art on Tyneside" exhibit was "re-created as a period setting for the objects—for example, the hallway of a grand house, a coffee shop, a picturesque ruin, and a craft workshop. Mannequins, smells, background soundtracks and interactives animate the displays" (Millard 2002, 493). These interactive exhibits include felt boards where children are encouraged to arrange architectural features such as plinths and columns to create their own buildings. This innovative approach to art interpretation has attracted a wide audience base, and visitor numbers have doubled in the ten years since it was introduced (Millard 2002).

Providing background information on the artist is also important, as this makes the art "come to life." To give you an example, simply labeling a sketch "Pencil Sketch, c. 1961, R. Bailey, Tavurvur volcano, PNG" has less appeal than "This pencil sketch shows the view from Rebecca Bailey's house in Rabaul, Papua New Guinea, where she lived

from 1955 to 1962. The volcano depicted, Tavurvur, erupted in 1999, totally destroying the town, including Rebecca's house." The second sign works better because it personalizes the drawing—some visitors may even remember seeing the eruption on TV and could use the sketch to imagine what the volcano would have looked like prior to the event.

Perhaps more than at any other interpretive site, fatigue is a key factor in cutting short visits to art galleries. Galleries have tended to exacerbate this trend by hanging paintings all at the same height and using small labels so as not to distract from the paintings themselves (Wright 1989). Although this may make sense from an aesthetic viewpoint, from an interpretive viewpoint it is unlikely to be successful. As interpreters, we need to be more creative and ask ourselves how we can make the visit "come alive" for our visitors. Providing background information as suggested above would be one way, but perhaps you could also develop interactive experiences. For example, visitors could be asked to search for objects depicted in paintings, guess when artwork was done based on the topics/furnishings depicted, compare two different styles of painting/drawing/sculpture, examine the artists' use of light, and so on. In addition to exhibit labels and signage, you could design workshop areas where visitors can try particular techniques (watercolor painting, sketching, and making collages) for themselves. Alternatively, you could introduce an artist-in-residence program that allows visitors to watch artists at work or participate in art classes.

All of the approaches suggested above make art more accessible and help visitors to learn about and appreciate the skills and expertise involved in creating "masterpieces." The key for effective art interpretation is to provide visitors with the opportunity to view the world through the eyes of the artist. It is

Trevor LYONS
born Australia 1945 died Australia 1990
Vietnam 1967-68

Journeys in my head: First state
1987 Brisbane
etching with aquatint on paper

Australian War Memorial, Canberra (45085)
A National Gallery of Australia Travelling Exhibition

Trevor Lyons served in the Australian Army in the Vietnam War from 1967 to 1968. He was severely injured by a landmine and underwent major facial reconstructive surgery. Twenty years later, Lyons made *Journeys in My Head,* a suite of 22 self portrait etchings, reflecting on the ongoing physical and psychological effects of his war service.

Figure 7.3. Making art more accessible

hoped that, in the same way that cases upon cases of specimens with tiny labels are no longer acceptable in museums, presenting works of art with minimal signage will also eventually become passé.

All for One and One for All: Improving Access to Signs and Exhibits

One of the main challenges for designers of visitor spaces and attractions is to ensure that exhibits and signs are equally accessible and rewarding for all members of the community. Simply providing ramps and restroom facilities for the disabled is no longer an adequate response to this requirement, particularly as the term *disability* covers a wide variety of conditions, ranging from those who are temporarily on crutches or permanently confined to wheelchairs to those who are hearing, sight, or intellectually impaired (Ryden and Bumpas 1996). Enhancing accessibility is not the same as "dumbing down" your exhibits and signs. Rather, aim to appeal to audiences with a range of learning patterns and abilities by developing creative, multisensory experiences with multiple entry points (Majewski and Bunch 1998).

Comprehensive specifications for catering to specific disabilities are listed in the

Americans with Disabilities Act (ADA). The main issues facing interpreters will be briefly discussed in the following sections; however, we strongly advise you to use the latest ADA standards as a guideline whenever planning and designing interpretive sites and activities. These are available at www.usdoj.gov/crt/ada/stdspdf.htm.

Removing Physical Barriers

The main difficulties faced by those who are physically disabled relate to access, not only to the building but also to signs and exhibits. Ramps, elevators, and handrails have become commonplace, but it is also important to ensure that the paths and access corridors through exhibits and attractions are wide enough to accommodate wheelchairs. Entrances to exhibits should be level if possible, and any changes in gradient should be clearly delineated, either by a contrast in color or by texture. Floor coverings, handrails, and ramps should be nonslippery, and any carpet should be made of a short, nondirectional pile (Miles et al. 1988). These provisions will not only help the physically disabled, but will also benefit other visitors, such as parents with strollers, elderly visitors,

Figure 7.4. Tactile models appeal to the sighted and visually impaired alike.

and those with heart conditions or restricted mobility.

It is important to remember that the physically disabled have the same reading level and interests as other visitors; therefore it is *access* to regular exhibits rather than designing separate or special exhibits that should be the focus of attention. In particular, it is important that all signs, exhibits, instructions, and interactive activities be visible and accessible from wheelchair height (Miles et al. 1988). Viewing heights of standing adults are generally between forty-three and sixty-seven inches (109 and 170 centimeters), whereas the eye level of those in wheelchairs is between forty and fifty-two inches (102 and 132 centimeters). You need to mount exhibit objects and signs low enough to be visible from this height and ensure that interactive exhibits are reachable and comfortable to use from a seated position (Johnson 2002).

"Painting Pictures"
Using Senses Other Than Sight

Early efforts to accommodate visually impaired visitors relied on using Braille signs (Fuller 1996); however, only a small percentage of visually impaired people can actually read this form of text. If you do decide to use this format, make sure it is mounted at an angle rather than horizontally, as this will make it easier to use (Hooper-Greenhill 1994). More recent approaches to catering to visual impairment focus on providing displays and exhibits that are tactile and three-dimensional, as well as models and full-scale replicas of display items that can be handled (Fuller 1996; Hooper-Greenhill 1994; Stapf 1999). Tactile graphics are particularly useful for map displays, as they enable designers to depict borders and areas using raised lines and different textures. These not only give visually impaired visitors an understanding of the display, but also create an additional dimension that all visitors will enjoy (Fuller

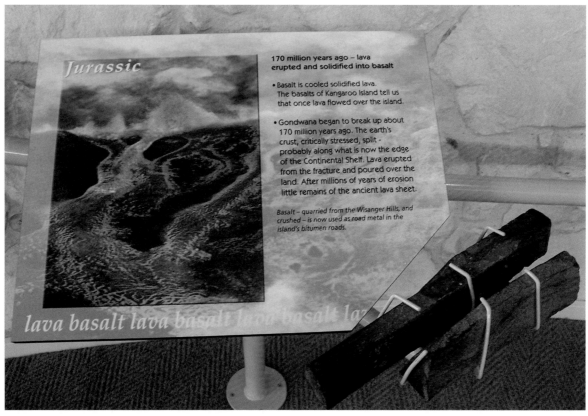

Figure 7.5. Something to touch as well as something to read

1996). In fact, tactile signs and exhibits are especially good for capturing the interest and imagination of younger visitors, regardless of their cognitive, physical, and social abilities (Johnson 2002).

When designing for visually impaired audiences, try to concentrate on portraying the most important elements of your exhibit or sign. These elements should be depicted in a format that is simple enough to avoid confusion and robust enough to withstand constant handling (Fuller 1996). A model of a railroad yard could include tracks, model trains, and platforms, for example; but fragile items such as signals and anything with sharp edges should be omitted. Fuller (1996) also recommends that wherever possible, designers incorporate easy-to-clean surfaces and materials that convey how the object really feels (such as bark for trees, metal for metal objects).

The same principles apply to replicas—not only do they need to be relevant, educational, and safe, they also have to be durable and regularly maintained. The range of replicas on the market today is enormous—skulls, scat, plants, animals, rocks, jewelry—and in many cases these look remarkably similar to the real thing (Merriman and Brochu 2005). Replicas appeal to all audiences because they give visitors the opportunity to get "up close and personal" to objects that are generally too precious to be handled. However, if you are using replicas, it is important to say so—never trick your visitors into thinking they have touched an original (Merriman and Brochu 2005). Visitors do pay close attention to detail and will expect items to be authentic if they are presented as such.

Some visually impaired people may have partial sight, and for these visitors strong color contrasts, uniform lighting, and large text will be particularly helpful (Hooper-Greenhill 1994). Magnification aids, such as handheld magnifying glasses, may also be

useful. Regardless of the degree of impairment, all visually handicapped visitors benefit from auditory information, such as portable sound cassettes or in situ audio presentations. This auditory input should be detailed enough to provide visitors with a clear mental image of the items or concepts being interpreted. Likewise, if interpretation relies on computer or audiovisual materials, the audio component should clearly describe what is being shown on the screen (Open Training and Education Network 1995). Where appropriate, auditory information can be augmented by odors to create a richer sensory environment—consider using leather and fresh hay to invoke images of a barn, or machinery and oil to portray a workshop. If you want to test how well your sounds, smells, and tactile components are working, try blindfolding potential visitors and taking them through your exhibit. Does their first blindfolded experience match their subsequent sighted tour, or are there gaps?

You can also make your signs and exhibits "come alive" for visually impaired visitors by amplifying relevant sounds. For example, Ryden and Bumpas (1996) suggest exaggerating simple sounds, such as the click of a bicycle wheel or the "whuunh" sound of a horse breathing as it works. Alternatively, you can use the universal language of music to contextualize your exhibit. Certain songs or styles of music can be used to portray an era (Elvis for the 1950s, the Beatles for the 1960s, etc.), and rhythm and tempo create moods (e.g., jazz sets the scene for celebrations and activity; slow classical music could be used to portray the movement of large rivers or decline of an animal species).

Songs with catchy tunes are a great medium for helping people remember messages—think of all those television and radio commercials with repetitive jingles that you simply can't get out of your head no matter how hard you try! Perhaps you could harness this by setting your interpretive messages to

Figure 7.6. Listening as well as looking

catchy or well-known tunes (Knudson et al. 2003). Music is also a powerful interpretive tool because we tend to associate a piece of music with certain events and emotions. For instance, tunes played on a bugle stirs images of war, suffering, and sadness; "Happy Birthday" evokes a sense of fun and celebration; and national anthems stir feelings of patriotism and pride. If used appropriately, these songs or pieces of music will attract visitors' interest and add depth to your interpretation. All the techniques mentioned not only aid the understanding of visually impaired people, but will also enrich the experiences of all your visitors.

"Making Music" without Sound

The main difficulty experienced by those with hearing impairment is the ability to receive, comprehend, and convey thoughts and ideas in an oral format. This particularly applies in cases where the hearing loss is congenital, as the impairment often affects the development of language, which itself is the basis for oral communication (Leigh, Cummins, and Shaw 1992). Thus, most (but certainly not all) people with substantial hearing impairment will experience difficulty with language abilities and/or oral communication, especially if they acquired the impairment at an early age.

Many hearing impaired people use sign language and written language to compensate for their difficulties in communicating orally. According to Leigh et al. (1992), it is likely that hearing impaired individuals will use more than one communication channel (speech, lip-reading, sign language, and writing), and that the preferred method of communication may vary according to the individual and the situation. Essentially, though, catering to hearing impaired visitors involves ensuring that any information presented audibly is also presented visually. If possible, audiovisual displays should be clearly subtitled. Captioning videos not only helps deaf and hard-of-hearing visitors, but is useful for all visitors when there is competing noise or crowds (Johnson 2002). If using holograms or other oral interpretive tools that cannot be subtitled, it is important to facilitate lip-reading by arranging lighting so it falls directly on the face of the speaker (Leigh et al. 1992). Words should be spoken clearly and slowly, but should not be exaggerated, as this makes it harder to lip-read. Also be aware that hearing impaired visitors may not hear subtle cues that indicate sentence structure, such as raising one's voice at the end of a sentence to indicate the sentence is a question rather than a statement (Open Training and Education Network 1995). If you want visitors to answer questions, you need to clearly indicate this through visual cues as well as oral ones. For a detailed discussion on designing and developing exhibits for and about the deaf community we suggest you refer to Kalisher (1998).

Visual cues such as diagrams, pictures, and dramatizations are useful additions to displays that rely on sound to convey meaning (Hooper-Greenhill 1994). Keep in mind that many hearing impaired visitors wear hearing aids. Because these amplify all sound, not just the sounds that are relevant to the interpretation, the level of background noise (from other exhibits, traffic, other visitors) needs to be minimized. According to Leigh et al. (1992), sounds that are loud or close to visitors will be magnified and may drown out more distant (and possibly more important) sounds. Indeed, even relatively quiet background noise may prevent those with hearing aids from hearing speech. Thus, you need to consider the possible negative effects of room acoustics, adjacent exhibits, and background noise as part of the overall design planning.

If possible, install signs and exhibits that are essential to understanding the topic, site, or feature where interference from competing sources is minimized.

Overcoming Learning Difficulties

The term *learning difficulties* refers to an enormously wide range of conditions that are neither clearly defined nor static. These conditions are often viewed as a continuum, where an individual may have difficulties with activities based on reading and logical understanding, for example, but may excel in other areas such as art or dance (Pearson and Aloysius 1994). The challenge for interpreters, therefore, is to present information in a manner that provides enjoyable and meaningful learning experiences for visitors with a diverse range of intellectual abilities.

Designing signs and exhibits that are easy to understand and require generic skills are important elements of this process. The motto "Less is more" certainly applies here, as visitors with learning difficulties will struggle if your signs have excessive text or your interactive exhibits are too intricate. This means that signs should be short, simply worded, and include explanations of any technical terms. Techniques used to cater to visually impaired visitors (large print, simple graphics, attention to color contrasts, and lighting) will also be particularly effective for this group (Pearson and Aloysius 1994).

Because there is such a wide range of learning difficulties, it is unlikely that one particular style of exhibit or sign will engage all visitors. However, if you design multisensory signs and exhibits (e.g., audiovisual presentations; things visitors can touch, smell, taste) and provide a variety of activities (e.g., dance, drama, mime, drawing, and crafts), you should be able to connect to almost all visitors in some way. If your site attracts school groups, giving teachers preparatory material such as replicas or posters of paintings/models/objects that will be viewed during the visit is invaluable (Pearson and Aloysius 1994).

As with all signs and exhibits, the key to success is to evaluate them with the target audience before, during, and after construction. You may *think* you've catered to specific disabilities and challenges, but it is often difficult for people with full use of all senses to isolate input from one particular source. The value of inviting your target audience to test your interpretation is illustrated by Fuller (1996), who designed a tactile exhibit using textures she thought felt distinct. However, when visually impaired people tested the exhibit, the differences turned out to be predominantly visual, not tactile. Had she installed the exhibit in its original format, its purpose would have been completely lost.

Appealing to Mature Audiences

As adults age, they experience mild to moderate declines in certain visual and cognitive abilities. Older adults often have difficulty distinguishing fine details, and are particularly susceptible to glare (Kelly, Savage, Landman, and Tonkin 2002; Morrell and Echt 2001). Many of the design features that cater to visitors with disabilities will also enrich older adults' experiences; however, there are several requirements specific to this group that should be considered.

First, as mentioned, many older adults have difficulty with glare; you should therefore position lights so there is minimal reflection from signage, displays, and protective glass shields (Morrell and Echt 2001). Second, older visitors find signs and images with little contrast harder to distinguish than those with high contrast (e.g., black objects on a white surface or vice versa). In addition, blues, greens, and pastels are less distinct than reds and oranges (Grinder and McCoy 1985). Third, the size and arrangement of text affect legibility, with research showing that double-spaced, 12- to 14-point type is

the most suitable for older visitors (Morrell and Echt 2001). Fourth, older adults are slower at adjusting from light to dark areas (Kelly et al. 2002; Whitehouse 1999); consequently, exhibition areas should be designed so visitors gradually move from light to dark. Fifth, older visitors often have difficulty processing auditory information when there is background noise. They find it difficult to concentrate and absorb information in noisy surroundings, so reduce sources of competing noises if at all possible (Kelly et al. 2002). It may even be best to use personal auditory equipment in some areas, as in Figure 7.6 (Silverstein 2001).

The physical fitness and agility of older visitors will also vary widely, with many in this age group unable to walk or stand for long periods (Kelly et al. 2002). Try to provide seats with backrests, particularly at interactive exhibits, viewing platforms, and areas where considerable time may be required to read signage or view exhibits. Many people in this age group also dislike crowds, and some may feel threatened in crowded exhibition areas. Designing quiet areas away from noisy family groups for reflective thinking will be appreciated, particularly if older adults are pursuing topics of personal interest or visiting with peers (Kelly et al. 2002). If your interpretive sign or exhibit is interactive, you also need to ensure that older visitors have the time and space to complete activities at their own pace. Also remember that older adults may find it difficult or even impossible to bend down to read signs or manipulate interactive displays. Consequently, you may need to modify exhibits that require agility and flexibility (Kelly et al. 2002; Reich and Borun 2001).

In addition to physical degeneration, there is evidence that some cognitive abilities, such as working memory and simultaneously maintaining and processing new information, decrease with age (Morrell and Echt 2001). Despite this, the ability to learn and interact with exhibits often remains unaffected (Grinder and McCoy 1985). Research by Kelly et al. (2002) reveals that older adults visit museums either to extend their knowledge about current interests or to discover new things. Thus, like most visitors, older adults expect to encounter new information and experiences that reinforce their values and remind them of shared histories.

Older visitors bring with them myriad experiences and will particularly appreciate interpretation that focuses on objects, places, and events with which they are familiar (Hein and Alexander 1998). According to Beck and Cable (2002, 67), "Seniors have a strong intrinsic interest in subjects dealing with the past." Several topics of widespread interest to adults over sixty-five have been identified by the National Museum of Australia and the Australian Museum (Kelly et al. 2002). These include health and well-being, history, the natural world, family history, art and creativity, and religion and spiritual practice. You could present these topics by focusing on activities, images, and experiences that involve and engage older adults. Exhibits could include archival films and old photos of common activities, pastimes, and places; oral and written stories or reminiscences of other older adults; displays and exhibits that present memorabilia in context; and so on. Essentially, aim to present objects and signs in a way that enables older adults to make connections to themes that are personally significant.

Many older adults are repeat visitors, and consequently may require more in-depth information than first-time visitors. This particularly applies to nature-based activities, as this age group tends to already possess a reasonable amount of knowledge about flora and fauna (Bultena, Field, and Renninger 1992). Social interaction with others of the same age is also an important motive for this group—try to design activities that encourage and facilitate peer group learning. These can be open-ended and flexible, as older adults tend to have more time and fewer pressing commitments than other visitors (Beck and Cable 2002; Bultena et al. 1992).

As you can see, accommodating groups with special needs involves designing multisensory experiences and signage that is clearly presented and easily understood. Embrace differences in your target audiences and endeavor to include them in your interpretation. You can even focus on historical or famous people who triumphed despite their disabilities, as too often these differences or disabilities are hidden rather than highlighted (Majewski and Bunch 1998). For instance, how many art exhibits mention the fact that Claude Monet was virtually blind by the time he painted his last series of paintings? How many historical exhibits show Franklin Delano Roosevelt in a wheelchair? Wherever possible, integrate design elements into existing exhibits so visitors with special needs do not feel isolated and "different" (Miles et al. 1988). The advantage of this approach is that it not only benefits those with special needs, but also enriches the experiences of other visitors by encouraging them to use a range of senses (visual, tactile, auditory) to access exhibition content (Hooper-Greenhill 1994). If you address these issues with sensitivity and respect, and involve members of disabled groups in designing, testing, and validating your signs and exhibits, your interpretation will be truly accessible to all.

Key Points

"Hot interpretation" engages visitors' emotions and challenges their values. It can be used to interpret controversial issues, and often presents topics through the eyes of those who are or were directly involved in the event or topic. You can also encourage visitors to engage with your interpretation by designing multisensory immersion experiences that create the illusion that the phenomenon is being experienced *here and now*.

Some sites and topics require sets of signs rather than just one. As with all interpretation, it is important to develop a theme to ensure that the individual signs meld together to present a logical interpretive "story." Sets of signs should have some common elements (e.g., sign materials, borders, and fonts) to indicate that the signs are linked, but should not be so similar that they become monotonous.

It is important to ensure that your signs and displays are accessible to a broad cross section of the public. Some key requirements include the following:

- Ensure that there is sufficient room between exhibits to accommodate wheelchairs.
- Ensure that all signage is accessible from wheelchair height.
- Use multisensory interpretation to cater to visitors who are visually or hearing impaired.
- Design signs that cater to a range of learning abilities.
- Ensure that visual characteristics of signs do not exclude older adult visitors.
- Ensure that signs and interactive elements are physically accessible for those with limited mobility.

Chapter 8

Designing Family Exhibits and Signs: It's Child's Play—Or Is It?

The majority of visitors to museums and tourist attractions are families, and, as a consequence, the body of research examining family behavior in informal learning environments is steadily growing (Borun 2002; Falk and Dierking 2000; Kelly, Savage, Griffin, and Tonkin 2004; McManus 1994; Moussouri 1998). In modern societies, family groups range from the traditional nuclear family to single-parent families, blended families, extended families, foster families, and coparented families. Throughout this book we use the term *family* to refer to a social group that comprises individuals from at least two generations—these may not necessarily include children. In this chapter we discuss how to design signs and exhibits for families visiting with and without children.

Families That Play Together Stay Together: Social Interaction in Interpretive Settings

Studies indicate that regardless of their composition, families tend to behave in a similar manner in museum environments (McManus 1994). Most families are drawn to museums for their educational and entertainment benefits, and for many years it was assumed that these were both derived from the exhibits themselves. Recently, however, researchers have realized that much of the enjoyment families obtain from museum visits actually stems from interacting with other family members. Indeed, it has even been suggested that families use museum visits to strengthen family ties within a safe,

nonthreatening environment (Caulton 1998; McManus 1994). Not surprisingly, family visits tend to be highly social in nature—family members often relate objects to previous shared experiences, invite other members of the group to view interesting exhibits or participate in activities, tell stories and jokes, and ask each other questions (Baillie 1996; Dierking 1989). They use these leisure activities to discuss family experiences, develop shared understandings, and review family history (Falk and Dierking 1992).

The importance families place on social interaction suggests that visitor attractions should aim to provide experiences that are engaging, exciting, and fun, yet also friendly and comfortable. For parents, one of the main attractions of museums and other informal learning centers is the opportunity to occupy and interact with their children. Consider how many times you've taken children to their favorite haunt, not because *you* particularly want to see the interpretive center, exhibit, or playground, but because you know it will occupy and amuse *them*! Often adults visit museums to meet the needs of their children and provide opportunities to view, touch, build, and share in interesting surroundings (Hooper-Greenhill 1994). Indeed, interviews conducted at the Australian Museum and the National Museum of Australia in 2002 revealed that parents specifically chose these venues because they knew their children would enjoy them. They even stated that the provision of fun and engaging activities for children was an essential prerequisite to them visiting museums (Kelly, Savage, Landman, and Tonkin 2002).

Families visiting with children are highly likely to use interactive exhibits, and tend to engage in discussions, active participation, and play (McManus 1991). Research has consistently shown that family groups spend longer at exhibits with a participatory component, and that those involving interaction among group members are particularly successful (Kropf 1989). This highlights the importance of giving families problems they can solve together as a group, and providing an environment that encourages conversation and discussion (Hooper-Greenhill 1994). Try to design interpretive signs and exhibits that facilitate social interaction and encourage the sharing of information and experiences. In particular, base interpretive experiences on activities that encourage team communication, such as puzzles, quizzes, skill acquisition, and interactive games that will interest and involve the whole family (Falk and Dierking 1992).

Figure 8.1. Ideas for team communication

Simply providing interactive signs, exhibits, and games will not ensure that your family visitors "stay and play." You need to check the physical surroundings as well. Is there enough room for everyone to see what is happening? Are there enough seating areas? Is there enough space for everyone to physically do the activity? Is the area likely to be crowded? Exhibits that require people to file past or allow only one person at a time to interact with the display are not particularly conducive to group interaction. All too often in this age of computer exhibits and technology-based experiences, the benefit of interaction and discussion in promoting family learning is overlooked. Because computer areas are often too small to accommodate more than one user, the opportunity for groups to view and discuss what happens on the screen is virtually nonexistent. You can easily overcome this by enlarging computer spaces or providing computer experiences (such as games) that require more than one participant (Falk and Dierking 2000).

The quality and scope of family interaction can also be compromised by the design of the visitor space as a whole. For example, in areas with a definite traffic flow, families viewing an exhibit tend to move on when a new group arrives, regardless of whether they have finished looking at the display. In addition, families usually avoid displays that are crowded or surrounded by other visitors (Kropf 1989). The message here is simple—if you want families to access your interpretive exhibits and signs, they must be positioned in areas that will accommodate multiple groups.

Museums and visitor attractions are not only places of social interaction, but are also sites where families can learn together (Hein 1995; Kelly et al. 2002). Studies show that visits are generally successful when adults think the exhibits are entertaining and educational for children, and the children themselves are interested and engaged (Grinder and McCoy 1985; Hooper-Greenhill 1994). To support family learning, you need to design spaces that allow adults and children to relate to each other and provide signs, exhibits, and experiences that encourage adults to take on the role of guides and teachers (Wood 1995). Simply having adults present is not enough in itself to foster children's learning—both groups also need to be actively involved in the experience. Observation studies by Puchner, Rapoport, and Gaskins (2001) at the Please Touch Museum in Philadelphia found that this learning support, often known as scaffolding, is more common in some activities than in others. Activities likely to engage adults and children in mutual learning were those that allow adults to clearly see what it is they should and could do, those for which children need help doing things correctly, or those that require a script for the activity to work properly (in their study, buying things at a supermarket). If you can involve accompanying adults both physically and verbally, and make it clear what they can do with their

Figure 8.2. Spaces for children

children, they are likely to stay longer. The longer they stay, the more their children are likely to learn (Kelly et al. 2002). Thus, it is in the best interest of all concerned that you design exhibits with children in mind, and that you also cater to families' physical comforts by providing cafeterias, restrooms, seating, play areas, and reading material (Caulton 1998; Hooper-Greenhill 1994; Thomas 1994).

What about signage for families? Observational studies reveal that adults are more likely to read text than children, and that adults use signs and labels as direct teaching aids (McManus 1994). It is therefore important to write in a style that enables parents to answer children's questions quickly and easily. In other words, parents should not have to spend too much time and effort translating or simplifying information to make it more palatable for children. Not only is this frustrating for parents, it may even lead to incorrect information being given to the child. Hood (1989) cites researchers who have observed parents making up explanations that are erroneous because they themselves don't understand the text. To prevent this from happening at your attraction, you need to ask the question, "What would a child want to know about x, y, and z?" and design text and graphics accordingly. This requires considerable skill and attention to detail: "Presenting complex information to children requires a distillation process defined by integrity, authenticity, refinement, and an in-depth knowledge of the subject matter being presented. But not a dumb-down ... everything presented [must] be thoroughly reviewed, understood from many points of view at different levels of abstraction and accurate beyond reproach" (Vexler 2000, 308).

In particular, interpretive texts should be written in small sections with subheadings, as these enable parents to easily locate the information required (McManus 1994).

Many of the issues discussed above are included in the recommendations of the Philadelphia-Camden Informal Science Education Collaborative. This organization recommends the following for designing successful family exhibits and signs:

- Design displays so that families can cluster around and simultaneously view objects.
- Develop interactive exhibits that enable the involvement of more than one pair of hands.
- Include activities that are easy to use for both children and adults.
- Make sure that results are varied and complex enough to encourage group discussion.
- Make displays that appeal to different learning styles and levels of knowledge.
- Write text that is easy to read and understand.

Ensure that displays relate to the knowledge and experiences of the family group (Falk and Dierking 2000).

Perhaps the overriding requirement of any children's exhibit and signage is that the activity be purposeful and interesting—children are harsh critics and will not tolerate boring exhibits! No matter how important the content, unless it is presented in an interesting manner, children will chatter, complain, or simply walk off (Robinson and Leon 1992). So what do children enjoy, and what gets them mentally, physically, and emotionally involved in the interpretive experience?

Gotcha! What Grabs Children's Attention?

Children learn through participation and imitation, and as any parent will attest, are much happier doing rather than simply watching. Similar behavior applies in

interpretive settings—show children an item and almost all will reach out to touch while simultaneously asking, "Can I try?" You should look for ways to encourage children to interact with the item (artifact, concept, animal, environment, or whatever). You are likely to have more success with interpretation that is based on participation, humor, fantasy, provoking curiosity, and stimulating novel approaches to learning than you are with static exhibits. Remember, modern children typically spend a considerable portion of their leisure hours in front of TVs, PlayStations, and computer games, none of which are static. If possible, the response required of young visitors needs to be fairly obvious, as children rarely read labels before trying activities (Caulton 1998). Indeed, observation studies at the Kirby Science Center Experience revealed that in 98 percent of cases, children did not read directions unless told to by an adult (Veverka 2001). Furthermore, if they had to read complex directions in order to complete an activity, many simply walked away.

Figure 8.3. Children like doing as well as reading.

Other studies suggest that the picture may not be quite so bleak—although children rarely read labels first, they do sometimes read the text once they have interacted with the display (Caulton 1998). If this is indeed the case, it is important to provide graphics that clearly illustrate what is required so that when children approach your exhibit, they know exactly what to do. The key is to make the graphics themselves look fun so that they attract children's attention (Veverka 2001). These could be accompanied by text that discusses the purpose of the activity and the concepts being taught. Aim to write in a format that can be read by older children as well as used by adults to explain to younger children what is happening. Some interpretive centers go so far as to have a cartoon "mascot" or character to attract younger audiences—but be very careful with the illustration you select. The authors vividly remember overhearing a group of visitors referring to the mascot of the local science center as "Condom man," which we very much doubt is the image intended!

To gain insight into what really engages children, perhaps we should turn to children's museums, as these are specifically designed with their young clients in mind. The furnishings are built to their dimensions, and the exhibits are designed for easy access and viewing by children of all heights. Arguably the most exciting aspect, however, is that well-designed children's areas provide the opportunity for young visitors to make their own decisions about which activities and learning experiences they participate in. Children love having the freedom to explore, and will often try several things, then go back and repeat their favorites (Maximea 2002). Those of you who regularly visit zoos with young children will probably be familiar with the bribe "Let's go and see what else there is—you can come back and see the lion/tiger/snake again later!"

In terms of designing child-friendly signs and exhibits, the lesson from children's museums is clear—children like to feel they have a choice. If you rely on a strictly linear exhibit or room progression, your site is unlikely to win the "really cool place to visit" award from younger visitors. This particularly applies to very young children, who quickly become impatient and bored if forced to stand in line to see exhibits or participate in activities. According to Falk and Dierking (2000), designing places specifically for children and giving them choice give the area a magical quality that both energizes the children and facilitates collaborative learning between adults and children.

Regardless of whether children's interpretation covers a whole museum, a few exhibits, or simply a "Kids' Corner," you should aim to design meaningful activities that link to or clarify the topics, features, and exhibits being interpreted. All too often the development of hands-on displays has been championed without due consideration of whether these activities actually promote any

Figure 8.4. Making children comfortable

real learning. In other words, there has been a significant emphasis on providing hands-on features, such as pushing buttons and lifting flaps to find answers, but little regard for whether such features are in fact "minds on" (Hein 1998). This results in situations in which "a larger proportion tend to flit from one thing to another, stopping to press buttons and turn handles, and treat the Gallery more as an amusement arcade than as a source of scientific information" (Brooks and Veron 1956, as cited by Hein 1998, 142). More recently, however, museums and visitor attractions have begun incorporating activities specifically designed to engage young minds. These include activities such as problem solving, developing lines of inquiry, storytelling, craftwork, and applying ideas or knowledge to new situations (Baillie 1996; Hein 1998). The focus here is on gaining the attention of young minds and engaging them in meaningful learning experiences.

Horses for Courses: Appealing to Different Age Groups

Interpreters need to keep in mind that families are diverse and often comprise adults and children of different ages. As a consequence, signs, exhibits, and activities need to appeal to a wide range of interests and abilities. There are two different approaches to designing inclusive interpretive experiences. First, design child-friendly signs and exhibits by writing in simple language and targeting topics that will be of interest to children of various ages. In particular, try to anticipate and answer common questions asked by children, such as the following:

- What is this?
- How was this made/what is this made of?
- What is it used for/what does it do?

- How does it work/live?
- What is interesting/unique/special about this item/animal/place?
- How does this relate to my world?

The main advantage of this approach is that children are catered to in the overall interpretation and therefore do not require additional interpretive signs and labels. Young readers are rewarded for reading the signs because they understand the content, and parents have quick and easy access to information that should satisfy inquisitive younger children (Museums Australia 1998).

The second approach is more costly and time-consuming, as it involves designing separate signs that cater specifically to children. Once the core ideas and themes have been developed, it requires you to design signs, concepts, and problem-solving activities that are progressively more difficult for different ages. In most cases, the information is presented in "layers" so that text and problem-solving activities for different reading levels appear on the same sign (Gurian 1991; Habertsma 1999). Generally, the most basic level of information is written in the largest print, using language and concepts deemed appropriate for young readers. Different target audiences can be denoted through something as simple as color, where the color of the lettering indicates information suitable for a particular ability or reading age. As we mentioned in chapter four, be careful not to use so many colors that the sign looks busy or cluttered. An added advantage of a layered approach to signage is that groups other than children (for example, those who are non-English speakers or have less education) will also benefit from having information presented at various levels of complexity (Gurian 1991).

The Powerhouse Museum in Sydney, Australia, uses the following approach when designing child-specific signs:

Figure 8.5. Minds-on—not just hands-on

• Level 1: Use an illustration for the very young that connects the object to an idea (e.g., birds building a nest). The illustration should represent the object as the child sees it. Thus, if the nest is displayed from the side at a young child's eye level, the illustration of the nest should also be from the side.

• Level 2: Use a title that attracts those of early reading age (e.g., "Building a Home").

• Level 3: Use a simple lead-in sentence about the object/animal/topic. This often includes a question or invitation to participate. As a rule, lead-in questions are ones that children would ask themselves (e.g., How do birds make this pile of twigs into a nest?).

• Level 4: Provide information. This is a junior version of adult text that gives some information about the topic and is suitable for older readers as well as adults. It could be accompanied by a pile of twigs and an invitation for children to try their hand at building a nest.

Regardless of the approach you adopt, you need to take some key principles into consideration. First, take care to place signs at a child-friendly height to enable them to be read out loud either by adults or by children with basic reading abilities. Second, use repetition, as this both appeals to children and aids learning. Third, if you use color to denote different levels, make sure these colors are easily distinguishable (see chapter four). Finally, signs and interpretation should be written in a child-friendly tone. The use of humor, satire, and cartoons is particularly effective in making learning experiences enjoyable for children (Falk and Dierking 2000; Habertsma 1999), as are poems and unexpected wordplay. You also can use popular TV characters or formats, such as traditional TV game shows, to tap into the mind-set of younger visitors (Nostbakken 1997). Alternatively, consider designing exhibits that deal with children's lives in other cultures or countries and/or periods of history (Robinson and Leon 1992).

Because children think and learn differently from adults, understanding the developmental phases of childhood is fundamental to designing successful children's exhibits. Current approaches to interactive exhibits owe much to the work of developmental psychologists such as Jean Piaget and Lev Vygotsky, who claim that children learn by directly interacting with their environment, and that their style of learning follows key developmental phases. According to Piaget, infants learn by exploring their own motor and sensory skills. Later, as toddlers, they start to explore their place in the world. Once they reach preschool age they become less egocentric, and by the age of seven, children start to conceptualize and create logical structures that explain their physical experiences. However, it is not until children reach adolescence that they develop conceptual reasoning and understand abstract principles (Piaget 1970).

Subsequent research suggests that the transition from one phase to the next may not be as defined or predictive as Piaget claimed. Some children develop more quickly than others, and some may excel in one particular area yet lag behind in others. One theory that has risen to prominence is Howard Gardner's theory of multiple intelligences (see Smith 2002). This theory states that intelligence covers eight areas: (1)

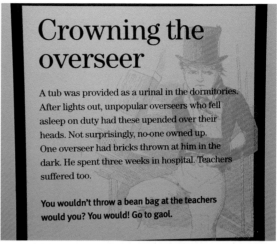

Figure 8.6. Using humor to appeal to children

linguistic intelligence (ability to use and understand spoken and written word); (2) logical-mathematical intelligence (ability to detect patterns, reason deductively, and think logically); (3) musical intelligence (ability to recognize and create music); (4) body-kinesthetic intelligence (ability to use one's body to solve problems or express oneself); (5) spatial intelligence (ability to perceive and represent the world in other media); (6) interpersonal intelligence (ability to communicate effectively); (7) intrapersonal intelligence (ability to understand one's own emotions); and (8) naturalist intelligence (ability to recognize and categorize features in the environment).

What does this imply for designers of children's exhibits and signs? Essentially, what Gardner and many others believe is that there is a range of intelligences, and that children may be more developed in some areas than in others. Although a group of children may be the same age, there is likely to be considerable variation in their strengths and abilities in the eight key intelligences. This means that to be effective, you should use a range of activities and presentation modes that encourage children to explore and learn in a variety of ways. Because you cannot force children to learn, you need to design experiences that are relevant and attractive enough to stimulate their desire to learn (Thomas 1994). The needs and general abilities of different ages, and the implications these have for the design of signs and exhibits, are discussed below.

Preschoolers

Children in this age group are eager to explore their place in the world. They have lots of energy and generally prefer to be active. Young children love to climb, explore, build, dress up, and role-play (Falk and Dierking 2000; Thomas 1994). Imagine their delight in finding a fairy grotto or a child-sized pirate ship complete with dress-up clothes, props, sounds, and smells! Such areas stimulate play but can also be used to enhance learning. For example, the pirate ship could have small sails that are hoisted with ropes, mock cannons that have to be loaded before they will "fire," a ship's wheel to "steer" with, hammocks to lie in, and so on. It must be noted, however, that preschoolers have limited fine and gross motor skills—avoid activities that depend solely on these (Falk and Dierking 1992).

You need to present instructions and explanations in simple steps, as children under five are generally comfortable dealing with only one concept at a time. For example, asking preschoolers to sort pictures of dogs into the largest and fuzziest would be very difficult, as they normally focus on only one variable at a time. Children under five are just beginning to understand the concept of cause and effect and are excited by the interpretation of simple relationships (Machlis and Field 1992). Your exhibit is likely to be very popular if it demonstrates the relationship between the child's action (e.g., standing on a colored square) and its effect (a noise). Be careful, though—noisy activities may annoy other visitors, as children of this age have a seemingly endless ability to repeat the same action over and over. One of the authors clearly remembers a museum exhibit that played the "Teddy Bears' Picnic" tune very

Figure 8.7. Learning while playing

loudly every time a button was pressed. After twenty minutes of nonstop "picnicking," every adult in the room was ready to tackle the next child who showed even a vague interest in approaching the button!

Another important thing to note is that children of this age have fairly short attention spans, so activities need to be short and "rewards" frequent (Beck and Cable 2002). In other words, the focus should be on exploration rather than explanation. At this age, actions are more important than content—try to include activities that require physical movement of some kind. If possible, your interpretation should also include elements of fantasy, as this sparks interest and involvement in children of all ages (Machlis and Field 1992). For instance, you could design exhibits and areas that encourage young visitors to playact historic events. This not only keeps them busy and amused, but helps teach them how and why historical characters behaved as they did (Beck and Cable 2002). According to Museums Australia (1998), children under five are generally not interested in videos and prefer spoken instructions to written text. They also love listening to stories and joining in with rhymes with definite patterns, such as those written by Dr. Seuss (1965). Using the same style, we have composed the following as an illustration:

> I'm strawberry jam
> I am! I am!
> I spread myself
> Because I can—
> On toast, on bread
> On Baby's head!
> All down her dress
> Oooo, what a mess!
> If you like goo
> Then I'm for you!
> I'm strawberry jam
> I am! I am!

Another thing to keep in mind is that safety is particularly important for parents of young children. For this reason, consider incorporating a central play area into regular galleries. This would enable parents to leave younger children in a safe environment within view while they accompanied older children through exhibits in the same gallery (Caulton 1998).

Early Primary

At this age children still enjoy displays that move and/or make noise, but they are also interested in the purpose of the display (Museums Australia 1998). They ask many questions, and are capable of reading simple explanations for themselves. Although children under six can summarize a day's events, they do not begin to grasp the concept of historical sequence until the age of seven or eight. Even then, matching dates with corresponding historical events and periods does not occur until the middle school years (Hein and Alexander 1998). This suggests that displays outlining the evolution of dinosaurs or the history of the California gold rush may be of little significance to younger visitors, and that concurrent child-friendly alternatives should be incorporated into the display. Thus, at the dinosaur display you could ask the question "How do we know what dinosaurs looked like?" and provide an activity that lets children don masks and brush away at a replica archaeological dig in which "bones" and "fossils" are hidden. You could design similar discovery activities in sandboxes or under piles of leaves. For interpretations of the gold rush, children could pan for gold using replica pans and materials that have properties similar to gold's. Indeed, the Sovereign Hill theme park in Ballarat, Australia, releases real gold dust into their creek and allows visitors to pan for and keep anything they find.

Like preschoolers, children in their early primary years are very energetic and eager to attract the attention of adults. Highly structured, passive exhibits are generally not very successful with this group (Machlis and Field 1992). Nevertheless, they do enjoy computer exhibits and will usually take the time to complete computer activities. They also enjoy competing with adults, and can often be seen using computers and other interactive displays with their parents

Figure 8.8. More spaces for children

(Museums Australia 1998). Peers are very important at this age, and children will often wait until others enter the area or activity before exploring. Check that your areas allow active participation by several children at the same time and that your signs and activities encourage group interaction (Thomas 1994).

Comparisons are important to early primary schoolchildren—signs and exhibits that ask them to compare and contrast are popular (for example, you could develop an exhibit on dogs that asks them to classify pictures of dogs using obvious characteristics such as size and color). Information that relates directly to them will also be well received. For instance, your dog exhibit could include a scale with weighted models

of dogs, and you could invite children to discover which dogs weigh more or less than they do. Opportunities to hone fine motor skills through drawing, puzzles, and rearranging items are also enjoyed by this age group (Kelly et al. 2002). As an example, refer back to the "Art on Tyneside" architectural features felt board described in chapter seven.

Children in the early primary years see the opportunity to introduce fantasy into virtually every situation and really enjoy exhibits with elements of fantasy (Machlis and Field 1992). Poems and stories that build on familiar tales will also delight— refer to books such as Roald Dahl's (1982) *Revolting Rhymes* for parodies of well-known children's stories.

Preadolescents

Children over eight have the ability to read labels for themselves but often prefer to ask for information. They tend to be fairly active and social in nature and, like young primary-age children, prefer learning in groups (Museums Australia 1998). Remember that at this age children differ widely in their development and abilities. However, most are able to clearly express their thoughts orally, and virtually all will have well-developed fine and gross motor skills. This age group responds particularly well to living history displays (Machlis and Field 1992), and will relish the opportunity to try on costumes, cook using old-fashioned kitchen equipment, pan for gold, travel in a stagecoach, and so on. Think back to living history attractions you may have visited—the most enthusiastic visitors were probably from this age group.

Preadolescents also enjoy sorting items into categories, and can cope with reasonably advanced classification tasks, such as sorting animals according to methods of reproduction or predation (Regnier, Gross, and Zimmerman 1994). They are able to form mental images and use these to complete tasks (Falk and Dierking 1992). You could, for example, show them a replica bone and be reasonably confident that they would be able to identify where on a skeleton the bone came from.

Adolescents

Peer group approval is particularly important to teenagers; therefore adult supervision and guidance tend to be less effective than for younger age groups. Generally, visits to museums and other interpretive facilities are not "cool," so it is your job to design exhibits around experiences and objects that are. Possible topics could include familiar modern technology (e.g., cell phones, computer interactives), living history, adventure experiences, and activities that encourage skill development (Beck and Cable 2002; Knudson et al. 1995). An exhibit in the Museum of Australia that is especially popular with this age group allows visitors to give a short oral presentation of their life history, which is recorded and then played back as if it were a television broadcast.

Typically, adolescent visitors cruise past exhibits in large groups, rarely stopping to absorb or discuss the content. However, it is not uncommon for them to follow this initial tour of the facility with a more careful perusal either alone or in small groups (Thomas 1994). As ideas and decisions are important to this age group, try to design signs and exhibits that incorporate opportunities for self-discovery and small-group discussion. The use of humor and satire for this age group can be more subtle, but should still focus on common adolescent experiences. Here's an example we've written to illustrate our point:

> Please run a Google
> On miniature poodles
> Oriental noodles
> The whole kit and caboodle.
> Find me some sites on
> Hong Kong
> The rubber-soled thong
> The history of song
> And why drainpipes pong.
> Then text me quick
> Or I'm going to be sick.
> Homework is due
> And I don't have a clue!!!

Although they are not the focus of this book, if you are interested or involved in organizing school-group visits to interpretive sites, you might find it useful to evaluate activities, displays, and signs with the Informal Environmental Learning Checklist (Ballantyne and Uzzell 1994).

It's a Small World: Designing Child-friendly Signs

The previous discussion highlighted the importance of designing signs, exhibits, and experiences that not only interest children but also have educational value. You don't need to spend lots of money to create effective interpretation for children; however, you do need to be reasonably creative and organized. Early design input is critical to ensure that children's signs and displays support the themes and purpose of the visitor attraction. Also, if you want children to read your signs, they need to be reasonably big. Museums Australia (1998) suggests that the following issues should be considered early in the planning phase:

- Are children an important segment of your target audience?
- Are there different age groups that need to be catered to (e.g., toddlers, preschoolers, school groups)?
- What interpretive techniques (interactive displays, computers, trails designed specifically for children and puzzles) will you use to appeal to children?
- Is it desirable and practical to have separate children's signs? Note that they take up display space, add more words, and can be expensive to produce because they often include illustrations. Early allocation of space and resources for the inclusion of child-specific interpretive facilities is important if they are to be effective.
- If separate labels are appropriate, where will they be placed and how will they relate to the rest of the interpretation at your attraction?

Although children's areas and activity rooms are becoming increasingly common, many designers fail to consider children's needs when designing exhibits and signs in other areas. Signs and exhibits are often too high and too complex for children (Habertsma 1999; Hooper-Greenhill 1994), and parents soon tire of lifting them to view exhibits that in some cases are very difficult to explain. Indeed, research shows that less time is spent at exhibits that are visually inaccessible to children, due to either dim lighting, exhibit height, or other physical barriers (Kropf 1989).

You can easily overcome these problems by displaying items at child-friendly heights or by providing a viewing platform for children to stand on. Alternatively, cut peepholes into the front of exhibits at different levels to allow viewing by children of different heights, or place transparent covers over holes in the ground that display models of various ground-dwelling creatures.

Children's Trails within Regular Exhibits

You can incorporate trails specifically designed for children into regular exhibits by placing appropriate labels, questions, peepholes, and tactile displays at child height within the overall display (Habertsma 1999). Wherever possible, signs and labels delineating the trail should be bright and eye-catching (Museums Australia 1998). You can also include discovery holes that children have to crawl into or numbers or letters that they have to search for to answer questions or puzzles. Because family learning experiences are collaborative, parents need to feel they are part of the discovery experience. Although they are unlikely to want to crawl inside a "discovery tunnel," they will want to be able to see their children and features of the exhibit so they can help the children use the exhibit properly (Falk and Dierking 2000). Accordingly, if you place clear plastic sheets at regular intervals (not unlike the playgrounds at McDonald's), parents will be able to locate their children and keep an eye on their learning experience.

Another popular activity is to include hidden objects within each display that children can search for. You can link these "detective trails" to question sheets that children answer once they find the objects. Alternatively, you could distribute pieces of a puzzle at particular points on the trail. Children can collect these and then assemble the puzzle to find the answers to the trail questions (Museums Australia 1998). Using a passport system and stamps for visiting certain areas is also popular. All of these activities enable family members to discover objects at their own pace and on their own level (Habertsma 1999). Although the scope of activities suitable for children's experiences is practically limitless, it is important to ensure that such experiences engage children long enough for the adults to assimilate the exhibit contents without having to rush along after them.

If the provision of a trail is beyond your budget, you might consider using a "discovery train" or "discovery corner," in which items of interest can be placed for children to access and use. Suggestions include replicas of the display items for children to touch, large wooden jigsaw puzzles depicting display items, activity sheets related to the display, costumes for dressing up, problem-solving games, and so on. Providing seating and reading materials for adults will ensure that if younger children want to play, adults also have something worthwhile to do (Thomas 1994). Alternatively, you could design family activity packs with separate activity cards for each family member to use and answer while walking around the site. You could include in this pack souvenir items such as postcards, pictures, and suggestions for activities to do at home that build upon the activities and experiences encountered at the site (McManus 1994). For younger children, providing a coloring table can be invaluable for occupying little fingers while adults assimilate exhibit information. Indeed,

Figure 8.9. Trails just for children

according to Wood (1995), anything that contributes to making the visit easy, pleasant, and fun could be regarded as an aid to family learning.

The principles and techniques described above can also be used to create child-friendly signs and activities in outdoor settings. For example, you could incorporate some agility, balance, and coordination activities into outdoor interpretation trails by using low-level balance beams, swinging bridges, climbing structures, and sliding track rides. This provides variety for the children and adds interest (even tired little legs often can't resist a challenge). Another possibility is to hide some "treasures," such as carvings, numbers, animal statues, or fake jewels (whatever fits within your theme), along the route for children to discover. Ensure that these are clearly pictured at the beginning of the trail so that adults as well as children know what they are looking for.

Children are highly discerning, are easily bored, and generally have a short attention

Figure 8.10. Back to the basics

span. Yet if correctly catered to, they are extremely loyal and will return to the visitor attraction again and again (Northey 1996). As families comprise a significant proportion of visitors to museums and other attractions, it behooves designers to employ techniques for attracting and maintaining the interest of the younger members of this very special group.

Key Points

Families visit interpretive sites for their educational, entertainment, and socializing benefits. Family groups are highly social, and members can often be observed relating the interpretive material to previous shared experiences, inviting other family members to view interesting exhibits or participate in activities, telling stories and jokes, and asking each other questions.

Successful children's exhibits incorporate some or all of the following design elements:

- Opportunities for physical exploration and discovery
- Activities to stimulate intellectual reasoning and development

Figure 8.11. Finding your own fossils

- Opportunities for problem solving
- Activities that encourage family/group interaction
- Interpretation based on a range of sensory experiences
- Varieties of color, texture, and movement
- Opportunities for individual reflection

Different activities and interpretive approaches appeal to different ages. Younger children appreciate the opportunity to play and respond well to activities that involve repetition, fantasy, and exploration. Children in the early primary years enjoy group interaction and activities that require them to compare and contrast items. They especially like signs that relate information directly to them as individuals. Preadolescents also prefer learning in groups. They respond particularly well to living history displays and also enjoy sorting items into categories. For teenagers, peer group approval is paramount. Ideas and decisions are important, and signs and exhibits should be designed to encourage leadership and self-discovery. Children's signs and activities can be assigned to separate areas in the interpretive setting or can be incorporated into regular displays through the use of trails designed specifically for children.

Chapter 9

Measure Twice, Cut Once: The Importance of Evaluation

Systematic evaluation allows you to measure the effectiveness of specific interpretive elements; to explore visitors' expectations, experiences, and satisfaction; and to check whether your site is meeting its stated objectives. Often, large sums of money are allocated to designing and installing signs, exhibits, and infrastructure, but little is put aside for evaluating how well these actually work. This is a serious omission, as bad news travels fast and disappointed visitors will be quick to criticize interpretive experiences that do not meet their expectations and requirements (Serrell 1996b). In this chapter we discuss the benefits of evaluating your interpretive products and present arguments for why this should be a fundamental part of your interpretive activities.

Is Evaluation Really Necessary?

It is true that evaluation can be costly and extremely time-consuming, particularly if it involves interviews and observation (Hein 1995). Perhaps this is why so few visitor attractions regularly conduct rigorous evaluation. As accountability and customer expectations change, however, so too do attitudes toward evaluation. These days an ever-increasing number of museums and visitor attractions are using a visitor-centered approach when designing exhibits, signs, and interpretive activities (Screven 1999) and insisting that their staff focus on the needs, expectations, and interests of their visitors

(Caulton 1998).

The main thing to remember when you design evaluation tools is that your visitors will have a wide variety of motives, preconceptions, expectations, and experiences. This will affect their learning, experiences, and satisfaction, as "meaning is not necessarily evident within the exhibition material itself. Rather, it acquires meaning when visitors relate it to aspects of their own experience and reasons for being there" (Ballantyne 1998, 84).

On the whole, visitors from similar backgrounds tend to share similar knowledge and conceptions. This means that if you gather information about the motives, knowledge, and previous experiences of your target visitor groups, you will be able to generalize about the range of conceptions they are likely to hold (Ballantyne 1998). You can then use this information to design exhibits that

- reinforce and build on accurate conceptions,
- "fill in" knowledge gaps, and
- correct common misconceptions.

You will find this approach particularly useful in front-end (prior to design) and formative (during design) evaluation, although in some cases it may be possible also to use it for summative (postdesign) evaluation. Each of these will be discussed and illustrated with examples in the following sections.

Getting the Ball Rolling: Front-end Evaluation

Front-end evaluation is used in the planning phase to determine the content, messages, and themes that exhibits and signage will incorporate. You can also use it to assess current visitors' views and preferences if you are considering renovations or changes to exhibits. Essentially, front-end evaluation examines the knowledge, interests, needs, and attitudes of your target audience (Bitgood and Shettel 1997; Screven 1999) and uses this to shape the scope and content of your proposed exhibit, signs, and activities. You will find this type of evaluation particularly useful for discovering how much people understand about certain terms and concepts—if the answer is "not very much," it tells you that you need to define these at the beginning of the interpretive experience (Serrell 1996b). The danger of not conducting front-end evaluation is that you could waste considerable time and effort designing signs and exhibits that interpret features, topics, or events your visitors either already know about or are not interested in (Woods and Moscardo 1998). In essence, front-end studies help you answer visitors' questions and ensure that their needs and desires are the driving force behind your exhibit design.

Because the main objective of conducting front-end evaluation is to inform the design and development of displays and signs, it is important to gather information early enough to influence design decisions (Hilke 1993). Some common issues you may wish to explore include the following:

- Who are my potential visitors, and how much time are they likely to spend at my site?
- Who are my competitors, and what information/experiences are they providing for visitors?
- What questions are my potential visitors asking about the topics/objects/ themes?
- What are my potential visitors' interests?
- What do my potential visitors already know about the topics/objects/themes I might interpret?
- Is this knowledge correct, or are there some fatal flaws/myths I need to address?
- How can my site best meet the needs and interests of future visitors?
- Are visitors likely to visit more than once, and if so, how can I design interpretation to cater to multiple visits?

Focus group interviews are generally the best way to conduct front-end evaluation because they allow you to "tease out" the perceptions, knowledge, and interests of prospective visitors. Using this approach, you can discuss a wide variety of philosophical and practical issues, and will generally obtain more detailed information than would be possible using more structured approaches (Knudson et al. 2003). Focus group interviews also allow you to use storyboards and illustrations to elicit responses about prospective displays and signs (Caulton 1998). Some researchers even record front-end focus group interviews so they have a collection of quotable quotes and anecdotes that can be incorporated into their final exhibits (Serrell 1996b).

Practice Makes Perfect: Formative Evaluation

Formative evaluation assesses the communication potential of exhibits and signs in their developmental phase. Generally, formative evaluation involves using mock-ups and prototypes to test whether particular approaches and methods are likely to provide viable signs and exhibits (Miles 1993). This method of obtaining information will enable you to test, revise, and retest inexpensive versions of your signs and exhibits until they effectively communicate what you intended (Bitgood and Shettel 1997). In other words, formative evaluation follows a trial-and-error format in which you test tentative interpretive solutions with potential visitors (Miles 1993).

There are many design issues you can test using formative evaluation. These include the readability, legibility, and length of your text; the clarity of your explanations; whether your questions and provocative statements engage visitors; the visual appeal of your graphics and illustrations; whether your interactive elements are interesting, appropriate, and robust; and where to position your signs and exhibits to maximize visibility and usage. Formative studies also allow you to observe how "nonprofessionals" access your exhibits and signs and whether they use interactive elements in the manner you intended. The more your prototype and its surroundings mirror the real thing, the more valid your measurement is likely to be (Thomas 1994). This means that if you are evaluating the effectiveness of a sign describing a Greek vase, for example, you should also place the vase (or a prototype) next to it (Punt 1989).

According to Bitgood and colleagues (1987), formative evaluation should include an examination of attracting power (whether or not people stop to read signs or use exhibits), holding power (whether or not people stand in front of signs or exhibits long enough to absorb the interpretive material), and knowledge gain (how much visitors have learned from reading signs or interacting with exhibits). You can measure this by installing paper versions of the proposed sign and observing visitors' spontaneous responses, then asking them a few questions once they exit the area. If visitors don't appear to be absorbing much information,

you may need to consider whether your expectations are reasonable. If they are, then you need to expend some effort in improving your interpretive content (Punt 1989).

Other issues you can explore through formative evaluation include whether your labels and instructions are clearly written and displayed, whether visitors understand the aims and objectives of each exhibit, whether lighting and other design features are suitable, whether interactive and interpretive elements are appropriate for the intended audience, in what order people use exhibits and how this affects their experience and understanding, and whether interactive elements will withstand frequent handling (Caulton 1998; Serrell 1996b; Veverka 2001). Veverka (2001) provides an entertaining description of conducting formative evaluation for a science center during which their "indestructible" microscopes lasted less than a week and most of their "visitors" ignored instructions for interactive exhibits.

You can see that not only does formative evaluation reduce the chance of making costly mistakes, it also ensures that your prototype is as close to "perfect" as possible prior to building and installing the final product. Some of the questions you can ask as part of a formative evaluation include the following:

- What do my visitors think are the main messages or themes being communicated by this exhibit/sign/display?
- Do the signage and interpretation make sense to my visitors? How do they relate to the more technical and complex concepts?
- Does the display address questions and issues that they find interesting, useful, or relevant?
- Do elements of the exhibit compete with each other, and if so, which elements are my visitors most likely to attend to?

- Are instructions easy to follow, and do my visitors use the exhibit in the manner intended?
- What parts of the exhibit attract the most attention and why? Are there any aspects that are ignored?
- Are my visitors focused and absorbed in the interpretive experience?
- Are my visitors comfortable in the interpretive setting?
- Do interactive elements fit in with the rest of the exhibit, and how well do they stand up to constant handling?
- Which way do visitors walk through the site, and is this the direction intended?
- Are signs clearly worded, visible, and accessible?

(Adapted from Fahy 1995; Serrell 1996b.)

The range of questions is virtually limitless, but it has been noted that no matter how many questions are asked during formative evaluation, you will never be sure exactly how well the whole exhibit works until it is actually installed and operating (Hein and Alexander 1998).

Tying Up Loose Ends: Summative Evaluation

Summative evaluation can be formal or informal, and includes a range of techniques, such as questionnaires, interviews, and observation. This type of evaluation is conducted on real exhibits and usually involves real visitors (Miles 1993). Essentially, summative evaluation involves examining signs and exhibits from a visitor's viewpoint to determine whether they effectively communicate themes and messages. As interpreters, we may think our signs and exhibits are clear and concise. However, summative evaluation sometimes reveals that exhibits convey connotative and conflicting messages and, in some cases, communicate

messages that were never intended or even considered (Miles 1993). As mentioned in the previous section, signs and exhibits should be evaluated "in situ" to give you a detailed picture of how well interpretive elements work in the setting itself. Signs may be easy to read in a quiet room with no other visual distractions, but may not have the same holding power in complex environments where visitors are moving through a range of exhibits (Pasini 1999). Keep in mind that despite the fact that summative evaluation is generally the easiest to conduct, any remedial action will be much more costly than if you had identified problems early in the design phase (Caulton 1998).

As with all evaluation, aim to design questions that visitors will find meaningful and that are likely to elicit usable responses. Simply asking, "Did you enjoy the exhibit?" tells you very little about what aspects were appreciated and why, what was interesting, what visitors learned, whether there were some aspects that were particularly good and some that were awful, and so on (Hudson 1993). In summative evaluation it is important to ensure that the questions are specific and are designed to elicit views on why and how particular aspects of your attraction work. For example, you could ask visitors to immediately recall specific facts, ideas, and concepts that were presented in the exhibit or to paraphrase the main messages and themes contained in the text. Alternatively, ask them to describe connections, identify implications, or participate in activities that reflect their understanding of the main message (Screven 1999).

According to Serrell (1993), one of the most effective ways of eliciting useful responses is to use open-ended statements, such as

- "I'm more aware of …"
- "It made me realize that …"
- "I didn't know that …"

This open-ended format prompts visitors to flesh out their initial reactions (Beckman 1999) and is ideal for tasks such as examining whether ideas are being effectively communicated or identifying which aspects of your exhibit, sign, or interpretive activity attract visitors' attention.

Open-ended questions are also especially appropriate for focus group interviews. If you decide to use this approach, you will need to gather together a sample of your target audience and ask them to verbally comment on the design and effectiveness of your signs, exhibits, and/or activities. Throughout this discussion you can probe participants' thoughts and emotions, teasing out issues of importance. Although gaining access to sample groups of visitors is often time-consuming, focus group interviews are very useful for providing an in-depth analysis of how your visitors perceive your interpretation, activities, and facilities.

Summative evaluation can also be conducted through formal and informal observation. Some managers argue that observation studies are a waste of time and that you can get a similar idea of how successful exhibits are by counting visitor numbers. Although visitor numbers can be used as an indication of an exhibit's success, these alone rarely tell the full story. Indeed, it could be that visitor numbers are essentially an indication of the success of the marketing campaign, rather than the exhibit per se. As Serrell (1993, 140) argues: "For an exhibition that is planned to capture, hold and direct visitors' attention, and to communicate messages visually and verbally, museums need data in the form of measurable visitor reactions, not just visitor numbers."

A number of authors have suggested that one of the best methods of determining the success of an exhibit or sign is to observe the amount of time visitors spend in front of it (Hein and Alexander 1998; Serrell 1993). Research shows that visitors spend little time looking at exhibits that are confusing or uninteresting, whereas those that are appealing attract and maintain their interest for much longer. Thus, it can be surmised that the more time visitors spend at the exhibit, the more attention they are paying to elements of the exhibit and the greater the chance they're absorbing and learning the material (Screven 1999; Serrell 1993). Serrell (1996b) argues that exhibits are successful if visitors move through the area at a rate of fewer than 300 square feet (100 square meters) per minute. She also claims that you can measure the success of your attraction by observing visitors' usage patterns—if the majority of your visitor sample attends to at least 51 percent of the exhibition, you can consider it a success (Serrell 1993). This figure is calculated by counting the number of possible element stops ("element" in this instance refers to a case, display, panel, sign, or interactive activity), then dividing the observed number of stops by the total possible number.

Observation is also valuable for mapping how visitors use interpretive spaces and identifying exhibits or sections that are being under- or overutilized. Wear and tear on carpets, trampled grass, and hand- and nose prints on glass barriers will all tell you which areas are being well used (Ham et al. 2005). Observation also allows you to pinpoint any bottlenecks or traffic flow problems (Hooper-Greenhill 1994), and provides a baseline measurement against which you can assess the impact of changing the content and placement of signs and exhibits. Essentially, informally observing visitors gives you insight into how they spend their time and how well your exhibits, signs, and activities are working. If, for example, you notice that several consecutive visitors fail to use the exhibit effectively or make similar mistakes, you can assume that either the exhibit or the explanatory signage (or both) require revision (Bitgood and Shettel 1997). Likewise, if your visitors seem lost or confused, or consistently ask staff the same questions, you should consider revising your directional and interpretive signs. Another easy way of exploring visitors' perceptions is to chat with them while they are looking at exhibits. Again, if they continually ask the same questions or express the same misconceptions, it gives you an indication of where interpretation needs improvement. You can even record these chats for later analysis or record your visitors' comments as they move through your exhibits (Serrell 1996b), although you will need to ask visitors for permission before you do this.

One of the best things about summative evaluation is that you can use multiple approaches to evaluation (Serrell 1996b). Thus, you can conduct exit surveys, interviews, and observations concurrently or consecutively, and combine results to produce an overall picture of the interpretive experience. Although summative evaluation is valuable in a range of settings, it does have an inherent problem in that visitors tend to say what they think you want to hear. In other words, rather than saying what they really think, they tell you what they feel they *should* think. Indeed, Hudson (1993) suggests that visitors often find it difficult to be critical of exhibits that have been lauded by designers, the media, and the public. He suggests that rather than relying on personal judgment, visitors tend to conform to the experts' opinion. This particularly applies when visitors have gone to considerable time and expense to visit the attraction, because negatively evaluating the experience is akin to admitting that they have wasted valuable time and money (Hudson 1993). One place where visitors do tend to air their complaints is in visitor books. Although these books provide a source of qualitative feedback for staff, they should not be your only form of evaluation, as they have limited validity and

are not statistically reliable. Indeed, according to Serrell (1993), visitor books are one of the most unscientific methods of measuring visitor responses and should be provided primarily for the benefit of the visitor.

The importance of conducting evaluation at all stages of design and implementation cannot be overstated. Evaluation is an essential aspect of any interpretive activity and should be factored into interpretive plans for both small and large sites. Unless you conduct regular systematic evaluation, you run the risk of developing products in a vacuum, without any clear idea of how visitor characteristics and exhibit variables interact to create positive interpretive experiences.

Key Points

Evaluation allows interpreters to check whether interpretive signs and exhibits match visitors' needs and interests; to ensure that themes, messages, and objectives are clear; and to explore what visitors are learning from their interpretive experiences. Front-end evaluation is used during the planning phase to explore the interests, motives, prior knowledge, and experiences of potential visitors. This information helps interpreters to select and develop the content, messages, and themes to be included in proposed exhibits and signs. Formative evaluation is used in the development phase to test, revise, and retest inexpensive mock-ups and prototypes of signs and exhibits. It enables you to make improvements and changes until the interpretation effectively communicates what is intended. Summative evaluation is conducted on real exhibits and usually involves real visitors. It is conducted "in situ" and is designed to elicit views on why and how particular aspects of your interpretation work. Summative evaluation can be conducted using questionnaires, focus group interviews, and observation techniques.

Chapter 10

Wrapping It Up:
The Interpretive Signs Checklist

In this final chapter we present a checklist that summarizes the main points made throughout this book. Based on the checklist developed by Ballantyne and Hughes (2003), it brings together the six principles of effective interpretation plus items relating to wording, formatting, and positioning of interpretive signs. We trust you will find it useful when designing new signs and/or improving existing signage. You may also like to refer to our interpretive signs Web site (Ballantyne, Hughes, and Moscardo 2002), which has a wide range of photographs illustrating "best practice" interpretive signage and can be accessed free of charge at www.interpretivesigns.qut.edu.au.

The Interpretive Signs Checklist presented here is designed to be used "in situ" either prior to or in conjunction with other forms of visitor evaluation. You can use it to evaluate a single sign or exhibit, or to evaluate your attraction as a whole. For ease of use, we recommend that you photocopy the following sections and take them around with you while conducting your evaluation.

1. Interpretive signs and exhibits are relevant to the intended audience.
    - Have you identified the main visitor group(s)?
    - Have you documented your visitors' likely interests and needs?
    - Have you considered your visitors' previous experiences and knowledge?
    - Is your information relevant for your target audience? In particular, does it "connect with" their previous

knowledge and experiences?
    - Does interpretation build on experiences your visitors may have had at other sites/attractions in the area?
    - Is your interpretation sensitive to the different social and cultural backgrounds of your visitors?
    - Does your interpretation take into account the needs and limitations of special groups (e.g., families and visitors with disabilities)?
    - Could some visitors (e.g., children and those in wheelchairs) have difficulty accessing signage and/or interactive displays?
    - Have you used metaphors, analogies, and personal stories to present information?
    - Have you used humor where appropriate?
    - Are your sentences short and easy to understand?
    - Does the level of language match the reading ability of your target audience?

2. Interpretive signs and exhibits have themes.
    - Have you identified the major topic(s)?
    - Have you developed core themes/messages based on the topic(s)?
    - Do core themes/messages focus on the special, rare, or different characteristics of your site or attraction?
    - Have you clearly stated your themes/messages?

- Have you supported your themes/ messages with stories and information?
- Have you reiterated your central themes throughout the exhibit/site?
- Have you linked local activities or events (e.g., festivals, workshops, hikes) to your themes/site?

3. Interpretive signs and exhibits provide novel experiences and avoid repetition.
   - Is your content interesting, surprising, and/or thought-provoking?
   - Is the information presented accurate and up-to-date?
   - Have you included a range of presentation techniques (e.g., flaps, models, quizzes, audiovisual components)?
   - Have you incorporated movement, contrast, color, and/or extreme elements into your signage?
   - Does the interpretation require your visitors to use different senses (e.g., touch, smell, hearing)?

4. Interpretive signs and exhibits have clear, organized structures.
   - Have you used catchy titles to attract visitors' attention?
   - Is the content clearly organized into an introduction, a body, and a conclusion?
   - Have you included clear explanations of central terms and concepts in your introduction?
   - Does your conclusion clearly reinforce the messages and concepts discussed?
   - In your conclusion, have you suggested ways in which visitors can integrate new information into their daily lives?

5. Interpretive signs and exhibits facilitate visitor involvement and choice.

- Does your interpretation encourage visitors to solve problems and/or make decisions?
- Do your signs and exhibits ask visitors stimulating and appropriate questions?
- Does your content engage visitors' emotions?

6. Interpretive signs and exhibits respect the audience.
   - Have you written your signs in "layers"?
   - Are there any sentences that could have double meanings or be interpreted in a manner not intended?

7. Additional design issues
   - Are your font and size of text easy to read?
   - Is your text well spaced?
   - Have you chosen colors for text, illustrations, and background that match your signs' content and tone?
   - Do illustrations match and enhance your signs' content?
   - Are your illustrations clear and easy to see?
   - Does the placement of text and illustrations look balanced?
   - Do the construction materials reflect the "feel" of the sign/display content?
   - Are the materials durable enough for the intended purpose?
   - Have you considered the issues of maintenance, vandalism, and longevity?
   - Have you placed signs where your visitors will see them (e.g., in direct line of vision, at natural stopping points)?
   - If your signs aren't directly in front of your attraction, are they within easy viewing distance and clearly matched

to the feature(s) being described?
- Is there enough space for people to view signage in comfort?
- Have you provided seats where appropriate?

- Have you minimized reflection from natural and artificial light?
- Have you used colors that are appropriate for the available lighting conditions?

References

Adams, G. D. "Using Research to Guide the Development of an African American Exhibit." *Visitor Studies: Theory, Research and Practice* 5 (1993): 136–42.

Alderson, W. T., and S. P. Low. *Interpretation of Historic Sites*. 2nd ed. Nashville, TN: American Association for State and Local History, 1985.

Aldridge, D. *Site Interpretation: A Practical Guide*. Edinburgh: Scottish Tourist Board, 1993.

Arndt, M. A., C. Screven, D. Benusa, and T. Bishop. "Behavior and Learning in a Zoo under Different Signage Conditions." *Visitor Studies: Theory, Research and Practice* 5 (1993): 245–53.

Australian Bureau of Statistics. "Aspects of Literacy: Assessed Literacy Skills." Canberra: Australian Bureau of Statistics, 1997. http://.nsf/Lookup/NT00006682 (accessed February 2002).

———. "Australian Social Trends 1998—Education—Educational Attainment: Literacy Skills." Canberra: Australian Bureau Statistics, 1998. http://7551EA 164D95600CCA2569AD000402B4?Open (accessed February 2002).

Bacon, J. P., and M. Hallett. "Exhibit Systems for Reptiles and Amphibians at the San Diego Zoo: Dioramas and Graphics." *International Zoo Yearbook* 21 (1981): 14–22.

Baillie, A. "Empowering the Visitor: The Family Experience of Museums: A Pilot Study of Ten Family Group Visitors to the Queensland Museum." Paper presented at Museums Australia 1996 Conference, Sydney, 1996.

Ballantyne, R. "Interpreters' Conceptions of Australian Aboriginal Culture and Heritage: Implications for Interpretive Practices." *The Journal of Environmental Education* 26, no. 4 (1995): 11–17.

———. "Interpreting 'Visions': Addressing Environmental Education Goals through Interpretation," in *Contemporary Issues in Heritage and Environmental Interpretation*, edited by D. Uzzell and R. Ballantyne, 77–97. London: The Stationery Office, 1998.

———. "Interpreting Apartheid: A Museum in Transition." *Curator: The Museum Journal* 46, no. 3 (2003): 279–92.

Ballantyne, R., A. Crabtree, S. Ham, K. Hughes, and B. Weiler. *Tour Guiding: Developing Effective Communication and Interpretation Techniques*. Brisbane, Australia: Queensland University of Technology, 2000.

Ballantyne, R., and K. Hughes. "Measure Twice, Cut Once: Developing a Research-based Interpretive Signs Checklist." *Australian Journal of Environmental Education* 19 (2003): 15–25.

———. "Using Front-end Evaluation to Design and Test Persuasive Bird Feeding Warning Signs." *Tourism Management* 27, no. 2 (2006): 235–46.

Ballantyne, R., K. Hughes, and G. Moscardo. "Interpretive Signs: Principles and Practices," 2002. http://www.talm.uq. edu.au/signage/ (authors' Web site).

Ballantyne, R., and J. Packer. "Teaching and Learning in Environmental Education: Developing Environmental Conceptions." *The Journal of Environmental Education* 27, no. 2 (1996): 25–32.

———. "Promoting Environmentally Sustainable Attitudes and Behavior through Free-choice Learning Experiences: What's the State of the Game?" *Environmental Education Research* 11, no. 3 (2005): 21–35.

Ballantyne, R., and D. Uzzell. "Environmental Mediation and Hot Interpretation—A Case Study of District Six, Cape Town." *Journal of Environmental Education* 24, no. 3 (1993): 4–7.

———. "A Checklist for the Critical Evaluation of Informal Environmental Learning Experiences." *International Journal of Environmental Education* and *Information* 13, no. 2 (1994): 111–24.

Baron, R. A., and D. E. Byrne. *Social Psychology*. 8th ed. Boston: Allyn and Bacon, 1997.

Beck, L., and T. Cable. *Interpretation for the 21st Century: Fifteen Guiding Principles for Interpreting Nature and Culture*. Champaign, IL: Sagamore Publishing, 2002.

Beckman, E. A. "Evaluating Visitors' Reactions to Interpretation in Australian National Parks." *Journal of Interpretation Research* 4, no. 1 (1999): 5–19.

Birney, B. A. "The Influence of Social Groups on the Use of Selected Northern Shores Graphics at the Denver Zoo." *Visitor Studies: Theory, Research and Practice* 5 (1993): 234–43.

Bitgood, S., T. Finlay, and D. Woehr. *Design and Evaluation of Exhibit Labels*. Technical Report No 87-40c. Jacksonville, AL: Center for Social Design, 1987.

Bitgood, S., and D. D. Patterson. "The Effects of Gallery Changes on Visitor Reading and Object Viewing Time." *Environment and Behavior* 25, no. 6 (1993): 761–81.

Bitgood, S., and H. H. Shettel. "An Overview of Visitor Studies." *Journal of Museum Education* 21, no. 3 (1997): 6–9.

Blake, D., and E. Hamilton. *Text and Context: A Guide to Speaking and Writing*. Sydney: Longman, 1995.

Blakely, R. L. "Formulating an Exhibit Policy." *International Zoo Yearbook* 21 (1981): 1–5.

Bligh, D., and B. Brooker. "Exhibition Design," in *A Manual for Small Museums and Keeping Places*, edited by R. Robins, 85–108. Brisbane, Australia: Queensland Museum and Museum Association of Australia, 1992.

Borun, M. "Object-based Learning and Family Groups," in *Perspectives on Object-centered Learning in Museums*, edited by S. Paris, 245–83. London: L. Erlbaum Associates, 2002.

Borun, M., and M. Miller. "What's in a Name? A Study of the Effectiveness of Explanatory Labels in a Science Museum." Report for the Franklin Institute Science Museum and Planetarium. Philadelphia, PA: Franklin Institute Science Museum and Planetarium 1980.

Brochu, L. *Interpretive Planning: The 5-M Model for Successful Planning Projects*. Fort Collins: CO: The National Association for Interpretation, 2003.

Brochu, L., and T. Merriman. *Personal Interpretation: Connecting Your Audience to Heritage Resources*. Fort Collins, CO: The National Association for Interpretation, 2002.

Bucy, D. E. "Applying Communication Theory to Design, Location and Evaluation of Interpretive Signs." PhD diss., University of Idaho–Moscow, Department of Conservation Social Sciences, 2005.

Bultena, G., D. R. Field, and R. Renninger. "Interpretation for the Elderly," in *On Interpretation: Sociology for Interpreters of Natural and Cultural History*, rev. ed., edited by G. E. Machlis and D. R. Field, 88–95. Corvallis: Oregon State University Press, 1992.

Capelle, A. D. "Designing Quality Interpretive/EE Programs: Meeting the Expectations of a Sophisticated Clientele." *InterpEdge* 2, no. 2 (1995): 33–36.

Carter, J., ed. *A Sense of Place: An Interpretive Planning Handbook*. Inverness, Scotland: Tourism and Environment Initiative, 1997.

Caulton, T. *Hands-on Exhibitions: Managing Interactive Museums and Science Centres*. London: Routledge, 1998.

Chambers, M. "Is Anyone out There?" *Museum News* 62, no. 5 (1984): 47–54.

Cox, S. L. "Follow the North Star at Conner Prairie, Indiana: A Case Study in Controversial Planning," in *The Manual of Museum Exhibitions*, edited by B. Lord and G. D. Lord, 483–86. Walnut Creek, CA: AltaMira Press, 2002.

Cross, S. "The Tip of the Iceberg." *Interpretation* 3, no. 1 (1998): 12–13.

Dahl, R. *Revolting Rhymes*. London: Penguin Books, 1982.

Dean, D. *Museum Exhibition: Theory and Practice*. London: Routledge, 1994.

Denton, C. *Graphics for Visual Communication*. Dubuque, IA: William C. Brown Publishers, 1992.

Department of Environment and Heritage. *Public Contact Manual: A Guide to Effective Community Education, Heritage Interpretation and Extension*. Brisbane, Australia: Department of Environment and Heritage, 1998.

Dierking, L. D. "The Family Museum Experience: Implications from Research." *Journal of Museum Education* 14, no. 2 (1989): 5–8.

Dierking, L. D., and W. Pollock. *Questioning*

Assumptions: An Introduction to Front-end Studies in Museums. Washington, DC: Association for Science Technology Centers, 1998.

Earnest, G. E. *Interpretive Recommendations for the Eastern Lake Ontario Sand Dune and Wetland Area*. New York: New York Sea Grant, 1994.

Fahy, A. "New Technologies for Museum Communication," in *Museum, Media, Message*, edited by E. Hooper-Greenhill, 82–96. London: Routledge, 1995.

Falk, J. H., and L. D. Dierking. *The Museum Experience*. Washington, DC: Whalesback Books, 1992.

———. *Learning from Museums: Visitor Experiences and the Making of Meaning*. Walnut Creek, CA: AltaMira Press, 2000.

———. *Lessons without Limit: How Free-choice Learning Is Transforming Education*. Walnut Creek, CA: AltaMira Press, 2002.

Falk, J. H., J. J. Koran, L. D. Dierking, and L. Dreblow. "Predicting Visitor Behavior." *Curator* 28 (1985): 249–57.

Falk, J. H., K. E. Philips, and J. J. Boxer. "Invisible Forces Exhibition." *Visitor Studies: Theory, Research and Practice* 5 (1992): 211–26.

Falk, J. H., C. Scott, L. Dierking, L. Rennie, and M. C. Jones. "Interactives and Visitor Learning." *Curator* 47, no. 2 (2004): 171–98.

Fuller, R. "Please Touch! Designing Tactile Models and Exhibits for Visually Impaired Visitors." *InterpEdge* 3, no. 1 (1996): 28–31.

Graf, B. "Visitor Studies in Germany: Methods and Examples," in *Towards the Museum of the Future: New European Perspectives*, edited by R. Miles and L. Zavala, 75–80. Routledge: London, 1994.

Greenwood, T., B. Woods, and G. Moscardo. "Visitors to Flinders Chase National Park." Unpublished report. James Cook University, Townsville, Australia, 2000.

Grinder, A. L., and E. S. McCoy. *The Good Guide: A Sourcebook for Interpreters, Docents, and Tour Guides.* Scottsdale, AZ: Ironwood Publishing, 1985.

Gunn, C. A. *Tourism Planning: Basics, Concepts, Cases.* Washington, DC: Taylor and Francis, 1994.

Gurian, E. H. "Noodling Around with Exhibition Opportunities," in *Exhibiting Cultures: The Poetics and Politics of Museum Display*, edited by I. Karp and S. D. Lavine, 176–90. Washington, DC: Smithsonian Institution Press, 1991.

Habertsma, N. "Working with Families," in *Museum and Gallery Education: A Manual of Good Practice*, edited by H. Moffat and V. Woollard, 89–99. London: The Stationery Office, 1999.

Ham, S. H. *Environmental Interpretation: A Practical Guide for People with Big Ideas and Small Budgets.* Golden, CO: Fulcrum Publishing, 1992.

———. "Beware of Interpreters Packing Little Ideas and Big Budgets." Keynote presentation to the Interpretation Australia National Conference, University of Queensland, Gatton, Australia, September 28, 1997.

———. "Scotching the Myth." Address to Scotland's First National Conference on Interpretation, Edinburgh, 2002.

———. "Re: New Interpretation Article." Posting to discussion board, 2003. www.interp@lorenz.mur.csu.edu.au (accessed 2003).

Ham, S. H., A. Housego, and B. Weiler. *Tasmanian Thematic Interpretation Planning Manual.* Tasmania, Australia: Tourism Tasmania, 2005.

Ham, S. H., and E. E. Krumpe. "Identifying Audiences and Messages for Nonformal Environmental Education—A Theoretical Framework for Interpreters." *Journal of Interpretation* 1, no. 1 (1996): 11–23.

Ham, S. H., and B. Weiler. *Profiles of Tourists in Panama Canal Watershed Protected Areas.* Moscow, ID: Department of Resource Recreation and Tourism, 2000.

Hartley, L., and M. Trueman. "The Effects of Headings in Text on Recall, Search and Retrieval." *British Journal of Educational Psychology* 53, no. 2 (1983): 205–14.

Hein, G. E. "Evaluating Teaching and Learning in Museums," in *Museum, Media, Message*, edited by E. Hooper-Greenhill, 189–203. London: Routledge, 1995.

———. *Learning in the Museum.* London: Routledge, 1998.

Hein, G. E., and M. Alexander. *Museums: Places of Learning.* Washington, DC: American Association of Museums, 1998.

Heintzman, J. *Making the Right Connections: A Guide for Nature Writers.* Stevens Point: University of Wisconsin–Stevens Point Foundation Press, 1988.

Helms, R. M., and M. C. Belcher. *Lighting for Energy-efficient Luminous Environments.* Englewood Cliffs, NJ: Prentice-Hall, 1991.

Hilke, D. "Quest for the Perfect Method-ology: A Tragi-comedy in Four Acts," in *Museum Visitor Studies in the 90s*, edited by S. Bicknell and G. Farmelo, 67–73. London: Science Museum, 1993.

Hood, M. G. "Leisure Criteria of Family Participation and Non-participation in Museums," in *Museum Visits and Activities for Family Life Enrichment*, edited by B. H. Butler and M. B. Sussman, 151–69. New York: Haworth, 1989.

Hooper-Greenhill, E. *Museums and Their Visitors.* London: Routledge, 1994.

Hudson, K. "Visitor Studies: Luxuries, Placebos, or Useful Tools?" in *Museum Visitor Studies in the 90s*, edited by S. Bicknell and G. Farmelo, 34–40. London: Science Museum, 1993.

Hughes, M., and A. Morrison-Saunders. "Impact of Trail-side Interpretive Signs on Visitor Knowledge." *Journal of Ecotourism* 1, no. 2/3 (2002): 122–32.

Interpretation Australia. "What Is Interpretation?" Interpretation Australia Association homepage. www.interpretationaustralia.asn.au/aboutwhatis.htm (accessed November 2004).

Jacobson, S. K. "Media Effectiveness in a Malaysian Park System." *Journal of Environmental Education* 19, no. 4 (1988): 22–27.

Johnson, D. R., and T. C. Swearingen. "The Effectiveness of Selected Trailside Signs in Deterring Off-trail Hiking at Paradise Meadow, Mount Rainer National Park," in *Vandalism: Research, Prevention and Social Policy*, edited by H. H. Christensen, D. R. Johnson, and M. H. Brookes, 272–87. General Technical Report PNW-GTR-293, USDA Forest Service. Portland, OR: Pacific Northwest Research Station, 1992.

Johnson, K. "Exhibition Accessibility," in *The Manual of Museum Exhibitions*, edited by B. Lord and G. D. Lord, 134–41. Walnut Creek, CA: AltaMira Press, 2002.

Jordanova, L. "Objects of Knowledge: A Historical Perspective on Museums," in *The New Museology*, edited by P. Vergo, 22–40. London: Reaktion Books, 1989.

Kalisher, E. "Re-examining Diversity: A Look at the Deaf Community in Museums." *Curator* 41, no. 1 (1998): 13–35.

Kanel, V., and P. Tamir. "Different Labels, Different Learnings." *Curator* 34, no. 1 (1991): 14–26.

Kelly, L., G. Savage, J. Griffin, and S. Tonkin.

Knowledge Quest: Australian Families Visit Museums. Sydney: Australian Museum Trust and National Museum of Australia, 2004.

Kelly, L., G. Savage, P. Landman, and S. Tonkin. *Energised, Engaged, Everywhere: Older Adults and Museums*. Sydney: Australian Museum and National Museum of Australia, 2002.

Klare, G. R. "Assessing Readability." *Reading Research Quarterly* 10, no. 1 (1974): 62–102.

Knudson, D. M., T. T. Cable, and L. Beck. *Interpretation of Cultural and Natural Resources*. State College, PA: Venture Publishing, 1995.

———. *Interpretation of Cultural and Natural Resources*. 2nd ed. State College, PA: Venture Publishing, 2003.

Kool, R. "The Effects of Label Design on Exhibit Effectiveness." *Muse* (Summer 1985): 32–36.

Korn, R. "Self-guiding Brochures: An Evaluation." *Curator* 31 (1988): 9–19.

Kropf, M. B. "The Family Museum Experience: A Review of the Literature." *Journal of Museum Education* 14, no. 2 (1989): 5–8.

Lackey, B., and S. Ham. "Contextual Analysis of Interpretation Focused on Human–Black Bear Conflicts in Yosemite National Park." *Applied Environmental Education and Communication* 2, no. 1 (2003): 11–21.

Leigh, G. R., R. A. Cummins, and J. Shaw. *Basic Education Needs of Adults Who Are Hearing Impaired*. Melbourne, Australia: Adult, Community and Further Education Board, 1992.

Light, D. "Visitors' Use of Interpretive Media at Heritage Sites." *Leisure Studies* 14 (1995): 132–49.

Lumney, R. "The Debate on Heritage Reviewed," in *Towards the Museum of the Future: New European Perspectives*, edited by R. Miles and L. Zavala, 57–70. London: Routledge, 1994.

Machlis, G. E., and D. R. Field. "Getting Connected: An Approach to Children's Interpretation," in *On Interpretation: Sociology for Interpreters of Natural and Cultural History*, rev. ed., edited by G. E. Machlis and D. R. Field, 65–74. Corvallis: Oregon State University Press, 1992.

Majewski, J., and L. Bunch. "The Expanding Definition of Diversity: Accessibility and Disability Culture Issues in Museum Exhibitions." *Curator* 41, no. 3 (1998): 153–60.

Maximea, H. "Exhibition Galleries," in *The Manual of Museum Exhibitions*, edited by B. Lord and G. D. Lord, 142–66. Walnut Creek, CA: AltaMira Press, 2002.

Mayer, R. E., and J. K. Gallini. "When Is an Illustration Worth Ten Thousand Words?" *Journal of Educational Psychology* 82, no. 4 (1990): 715–26.

Mayrand, Y. "The Role of the Exhibition Designer," in *The Manual of Museum Exhibitions*, edited by B. Lord and G. D. Lord, 405–24. Walnut Creek, CA: AltaMira Press, 2002.

McArthur, S. "Introducing the Under-capitalised World of Interpretation in Ecotourism," in *Ecotourism: A Guide for Planners and Managers*, vol. 2, edited by K. Lindberg, M. Epler-Wood, and D. Engeldrum, 63–85. North Bennington, VT: The Ecotourism Society, 1998.

McEachern, C. "Working with Memory: The District Six Museum in the New South Africa." *Social Analysis* 42, no. 2 (1998): 47–72.

McIntosh, L. "When Is a Label Not a Label? Labeling Animal Life as It Happens." *Visitor Studies: Theory, Research and Practice* 7, no. 1 (1996): 41–47.

McManus, P. M. "Oh Yes They Do: How Museum Visitors Read Labels and Interact with Exhibit Texts." *Curator* 32, no. 3 (1989): 174–89.

———. "Making Sense of Exhibits," in *Museum Language: Objects and Text*, edited by G. Kavanagh, 35–46. Leicester, United Kingdom: Leicester University Press, 1991.

———. "Families in Museums," in *Towards the Museum of the Future: New European Perspectives*, edited by R. Miles and L. Zavala, 81–97. London: Routledge, 1994.

———. "Preferred Pedestrian Flow: A Tool for Designing Optimum Interpretive Conditions and Visitor Pressure Management." *Journal of Tourism Studies* 9, no. 1 (1998): 40–50.

Merriman, T., and L. Brochu. *Management of Interpretive Sites: Developing Sustainable Operations through Effective Leadership*. Fort Collins, CO: The National Association for Interpretation, 2005.

Middleton, J. L. "Student-generated Analogies in Biology." *American Biology Teacher* 53, no. 1 (1991): 42–46.

Miles, R. "Grasping the Greased Pig: Evaluation of Educational Exhibits," in *Museum Visitor Studies in the 90s*, edited by S. Bicknell and G. Farmelo, 24–33. London: Science Museum, 1993.

Miles, R. S., M. B. Alt, D. C. Gosling, B. N. Lewis, and A. F. Tout. *The Design of Educational Exhibits*. 2nd ed. London: Unwin Hyman, 1988.

Millard, J. "Art on Tyneside at the Laing Art Gallery, Tyne and Wear Museums, Newcastle," in *The Manual of Museum Exhibitions*, edited by B. Lord and G. D. Lord, 491–95. Walnut Creek, CA: AltaMira Press, 2002.

Morrell, R. W., and K. V. Echt. "Presenting Information to Older Adults." *Journal of Museum Education* 26, no. 1 (2001): 10–12.

Moscardo, G. "Mindful Visitors: Heritage and Tourism." *Annals of Tourism Research* 23, no. 2 (1996): 376–97.

———. "Interpretation and Sustainable Tourism: Functions, Examples and Principles." *Journal of Tourism Studies* 9, no. 1 (1998): 2–13.

———. *Making Visitors Mindful: Principles for Creating Sustainable Visitor Experiences through Effective Communication.* Champaign, IL: Sagamore Publishing, 1999.

———. *Rainforest Visitor Profiles.* Cairns, Australia: Rainforest Cooperative Research Centre, 2001.

Moscardo, G., and B. Woods. "Managing Tourism and the Experience of Visitors on Skyrail," in *Embracing and Managing Change in Tourism*, edited by E. Laws, B. Falkner, and G. Moscardo, 307–23. London: Routledge, 1998.

Moussouri, T. "Family Agendas and the Museum Experience." *Museum Archaeologist* 24 (1998): 20–30.

Museums Australia. *Museum Methods: A Practical Manual for Managing Small Museums.* Sydney: Museums Australia, 1998.

Northey, V. *Getting Them Young and Keeping Them: The Future of Children's Museums in Australia.* Report for National Museum of Australia, Canberra, 1996. Available online at http://archive.amol.org.au/evrsig/pdf/northey.pdf (accessed August 2005).

Nostbakken, J. "A Capital Change." *InterpEdge* 4, no. 1 (1997): 28–29.

Olsen, E. C., M. L. Bowman, and R. E. Roth. "Interpretation and Nonformal Education in Natural Resources Management." *Journal of Environmental Education* 15 (1984): 6–10.

Olson, J. M., and C. A. Brewer. "An Evaluation of Color Selections to Accommodate Map Users with Color-vision Impairments." *Annals of the Association of American Geographers* 87, no. 1 (1997): 103–32.

Open Training and Education Network. *Working with People with Disabilities.* 2nd ed. Sydney: The Open Training and Education Network, 1995.

Organisation for Economic Co-operation and Development. "Literacy in the Information Age: Final Report of the International Adult Literacy Survey, 2002." Paris: OECD. www.oecd.org/els/education/literacy/docs.htm (accessed February 2002).

Packer, J., and R. Ballantyne. "Solitary vs. Shared Learning: Exploring the Social Dimension of Museum Learning." *Curator: The Museum Journal* 48, no. 2 (2005): 177–92.

Parker, R. C. *Looking Good in Print.* Research Triangle Park, NC: Ventana, 1997.

Pasini, R. "Sign-posting Information Design," in *Information Design*, edited by R. Jacobson, 83–98. Cambridge, MA: MIT Press, 1999.

Pearce, S. M. "Collecting Reconsidered," in *Museum Languages: Objects and Texts*, edited by G. Kavanagh, 135–53. Leicester, United Kingdom: Leicester University Press, 1991.

Pearson, A., and C. Aloysius. *Museums and Children with Learning Difficulties: The Big Foot.* London: British Museum Press, 1994.

Piaget, J. *The Science of Education and the Psychology of the Child.* New York: Grossman, 1970.

Pierssene, A. *Explaining Our World: An Approach to the Art of Environmental Interpretation.* London: E. and F. N. Spon, 1999.

Prince, D. R. "Countryside Interpretation: A Cognitive Evaluation." *Museums Journal* 82 (1982): 165–70.

Puchner, L., R. Rapoport, and S. Gaskins. "Learning in Children's Museums: Is It Really Happening?" *Curator* 44, no. 3 (2001): 237–60.

Punt, B. *Doing It Right: A Workbook for Improving Exhibit Labels*. Brooklyn, NY: The Brooklyn Children's Museum, 1989.

Rand, J. *Fish Stories That Hook Readers: Interpretive Graphics at the Monterey Bay Aquarium*. Technical Report no. 90-30. Jacksonville, AL: Center for Social Design, 1985.

Regnier, K., M. Gross, and R. Zimmerman. *The Interpreter's Guidebook: Techniques for Programs and Presentations*. 3rd ed. Stevens Point: University of Wisconsin–Stevens Point Foundation Press, 1994.

Reich, C., and M. Borun. "Exhibition Accessibility and the Senior Visitor." *Journal of Museum Education* 26, no. 1 (2001): 13–16.

Robertshaw, A. "A Dry Shell of the Past: Living History and the Interpretation of Historic Houses," *Interpretation* 3, no. 2 (1997). www.heritageinterpretation.org.uk/journals/j2c-shell.html (accessed September 11, 2003).

Robinson, C., and W. Leon. "A Priority on Process: The Indianapolis Children's Museums and 'Mysteries in History'," in *Ideas and Images: Developing Interpretive History Exhibits*, edited by K. L. Ames, B. Franco, and L. T. Frye, 211–32. Nashville, TN: American Association for State and Local History, 1992.

Rogers, H. G., and F. W. Brown. "The Impact of Writing Style on Compliance with Instructions." *Journal of Technical Writing and Communication* 23, no. 1 (1993): 53–71.

Rudin, E. B. "A Sign for All Seasons: From Writer's Clipboard to Zoo Exhibit." *Curator* 22, no. 4 (1980): 23–25.

Ryden, K., and E. Bumpas. "Designing up to ADA." *InterpEdge* 3, no. 1 (1996): 56–58.

Sawyer, M. H. "A Review of Research in Revising Instructional Text." *Journal of Reading Behavior* 23, no. 3 (1991): 307–33.

Schauble, L., G. Leinhardt, and L. Martin. "A Framework for Organizing a Cumulative Research Agenda in Informal Learning Contexts." *Journal of Museum Education* 22, no. 2/3 (1997): 3–7.

Schiffman, L. G. *Consumer Behaviour*. 2nd ed. Sydney, Australia: Prentice Hall, 2001.

Screven, C. G. "Information Design in Informal Settings: Museums and Other Public Spaces," in *Information Design*, edited by R. Jacobson, 131–92. Cambridge, MA: MIT Press, 1999.

Serrell, B. "Zoo Label Study at Brookfield Zoo." *International Zoo Yearbook* 21 (1981): 54–61.

———. "Using Behaviour to Define the Effectiveness of Exhibitions," in *Museum Visitor Studies in the 90s*, edited by S. Bicknell and G. Farmelo, 140–44. London: Science Museum, 1993.

———. *Exhibit Labels: An Interpretive Approach*. Walnut Creek, CA: AltaMira Press, 1996a.

———. "In Search of Generalizability: New Tools for Visitor Studies." *Journal of Museum Education* 21, no. 3 (1996b): 11–18.

Seuss, Dr. *Fox in Socks*. New York: Beginner Books, 1965.

Shackley, M. *Visitor Management Case Studies from World Heritage Sites*. Oxford, United Kingdom: Butterworth-Heinemann, 2000.

Shaw, K. "Lighting," in *The Manual of Museum Exhibitions*, edited by B. Lord and G. D. Lord, 207–14. Walnut Creek, CA: AltaMira Press, 2002a.

———. "Lighting the Show," in *The Manual of Museum Exhibitions*, edited by B. Lord and G. D. Lord, 437–41. Walnut Creek, CA: AltaMira Press, 2002b.

Silverstein, N. M. "Museums and Aging: Reflections on the Aging Visitor, Volunteer, and Employee." *Journal of Museum Education* 26, no. 1 (2001): 3–6.

Slivovsky, K. "Rules of Thumb for Writing Signs." *Ribbit* (Spring 2001): 3.

Smith, M. K. "Howard Gardner and Multiple Intelligences." *The Encyclopedia of Informal Education*, 2002. www.infed.org/thinkers/gardner.htm (accessed February 14, 2004).

Society for the Interpretation of Britain's Heritage. "About SIBH." *Interpretation Journal* 50 (1992): 1.

Sorensen, C. "Theme Parks and Time Machines," in *The New Museology*, edited by P. Vergo, 60–73. London: Reaktion Books, 1989.

Sorsby, B. D., and S. D. Horne. "The Readability of Museum Labels." *Museums Journal* 80, no. 3 (1980): 157–59.

Spencer, H. A. D. "Balancing Perspectives in Exhibition Text," in *The Manual of Museum Exhibitions*, edited by B. Lord and G. D. Lord, 394–98. Walnut Creek, CA: AltaMira Press, 2002.

Spock, D. "Is It Interactive Yet?" *Curator* 47, no. 4 (2004): 369–74.

Staiff, R., and R. Bushell. "Travel Knowledgeably," in *Interpreting the Land Down Under: Australian Heritage Interpretation and Tour Guiding*, edited by R. Black and B. Weiler, 92–107. Golden, CO: Fulcrum Publishing, 2003.

Stapf, B. "Developing Educational Strategies and Support Materials for Children," in *Museum and Gallery Education: A Manual of Good Practice*, edited by H. Moffat and V. Woollard, 43–55. London: The Stationery Office, 1999.

Strauss, S. "The Passionate Fact: An Overview of Storytelling in Interpretation." *InterpEdge* 2, no. 2 (1995): 27–28.

Thomas, G. "'Why Are You Playing at Washing Up Again?' Some Reasons and Methods for Developing Exhibitions for Children," in *Towards the Museum of the Future: New European Perspectives*, edited by R. Miles and L. Zavala, 117–31. London: Routledge, 1994.

Thompson, D., and S. Bitgood. "The Effects of Sign Length, Letter Size and Proximity on Reading." *Visitor Studies: Theory, Research and Practice* 1 (1988): 101–12.

Tilden, F. *Interpreting Our Heritage*. 3rd ed. Chapel Hill: University of North Carolina Press, 1977.

Trapp, S., M. Gross, and R. Zimmerman. *Signs, Trails, and Wayside Exhibits: Connecting People and Places*. Stevens Point: University of Wisconsin–Stevens Point Foundation Press, 1994.

Uzzell, D. "Interpreting Our Heritage: A Theoretical Interpretation," in *Contemporary Issues in Heritage and Environmental Interpretation*, edited by D. Uzzell and R. Ballantyne, 11–25. London: The Stationery Office, 1998.

Veverka, J. A. *Interpretive Master Planning: For Parks, Historic Sites, Forests, Zoos and Related Tourism Sites, for Self-guided Interpretive Services, for Interpretive Exhibits, for Guided Programs/Tours*. Helena, MT: Falcon Press, 1994.

———. "Exhibit Evaluation for Children's Exhibits: The Kirby Science Center Experience." Okemos, MI: Veverka and Associates, 2001. www.heritageinterp.com (accessed May 2007).

Vexler, J. A. "Children's Museum Exhibits: Distilled or Watered Down?" *Curator* 43, no. 4 (2000): 307–12.

Volkert, J. W. "Monologue to Dialogue." *Museum News* 70, no. 2 (1991): 46–48.

Walker, E. "A Front-end Evaluation Conducted to Facilitate Planning the Royal Ontario Museum's European Galleries." *Visitor Studies: Theory, Research and Practice* 1 (1988): 139–43.

Washburne, R. F., and J. Wagar. "Evaluating Visitor Response to Exhibit Content." *Curator* 15 (1972): 248–54.

Whitehouse, R. "The Uniqueness of Individual Perception," in *Information Design*, edited by R. Jacobson, 103–30. Cambridge, MA: MIT Press, 1999.

Williams, T. R. "Text or Graphic: An Information Processing Perspective on Choosing the More Effective Medium." *Journal of Technical Writing and Communication* 23, no. 1 (1993): 33–52.

Wolf, L. F., and J. K. Smith. "What Makes Museum Labels Legible?" *Curator* 36, no. 2 (1993): 95–110.

Wolf, R. L., M. E. Munley, and B. L. Tymitz. *The Pause That Refreshes: A Study of Visitor Reactions to the Discovery Corners in the National Museum of History and Technology, Smithsonian Institution*. Washington, DC: Smithsonian Institution, 1979.

Wood, R. "Museums, Means and Motivation: Adult Learning in a Family Context," in *Museums and the Education of Adults*, edited by A. Chadwick and A. Stannett, 97–102. Leicester, United Kingdom: National Institute of Adult Continuing Education, 1995.

Woods, B. *Signs, Signs Everywhere, but Are They Being Read?* Cairns, Australia: Cooperative Research Centre for Tropical Rainforest Ecology and Management, 1997.

———. "Wildlife Tourism and the Visitor Experience: Flinders Chase National Park, Kangaroo Island," in *Capitalising on Research*, edited by C. Pforr and B. Janeczko, 377–94. Canberra, Australia: Bureau of Tourism Research, 2001.

Woods, B., and G. Moscardo. "Researching Interpretive Techniques in Tourism: An Evaluation of the Effectiveness of Pictorial Symbols in Reef Tourist Education," in *Progress in Tourism and Hospitality Research*, part 1, edited by B. Faulkner, C. Tidswell, and D. Weaver, 320–33. Canberra, Australia: Bureau of Tourism Research, 1998.

Woods, B., G. Moscardo, and T. Greenwood. *A Critical Review of Readability and Comprehensibility Tests*. London: Reaktion Books, 1998.

Wright, P. "The Quality of Visitors' Experiences in Art Museums," in *The New Museology*, edited by P. Vergo, 119–48. London: Reaktion Books.

Zehr, J., M. Gross, and R. Zimmerman. *Creating Environmental Publications: A Guide to Writing and Designing for Interpreters and Environmental Educators*. Stevens Point: University of Wisconsin–Stevens Point Foundation Press. 1991.

Index

Other interpretation books in the Applied Communications Series
Sam H. Ham, Editor

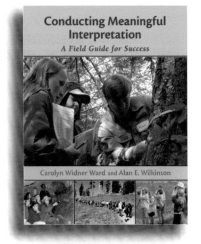

Conducting Meaningful Interpretation
A Field Guide for Success
Carolyn Widner Ward and Alan E. Wilkinson

This reference guide is a vital resource for guides and interpreters in natural resources management programs. Includes tips on traditional campfire programs, high-tech audiovisual presentations, presenting to special groups, and much more.

288 pages • b/w charts, graphics • PB $75.00
ISBN-13: 978-1-55591-530-8

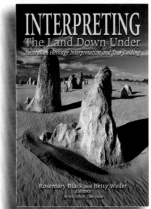

Interpreting the Land Down Under
Australian Heritage Interpretation and Tour Guiding
Edited by Rosemary Black and Betty Weiler

Australia provides an ideal setting for the research of interpretation, with lessons that can be applied around the world.

240 pages • b/w illustrations • PB $19.95
ISBN-13: 978-1-55591-865-1

Environmental Interpretation
A Practical Guide for People with Big Ideas and Small Budgets
Sam H. Ham

This is a diverse collection of low-cost communication techniques that really work. Simple instructions are offered for designing and implementing effective education programs in forests, parks, protected areas, zoos, botanical gardens, and all types of natural resources management programs.

486 pages • b/w and color photos, graphics • PB $49.95
ISBN-13: 978-1-55591-902-3

FULCRUM PUBLISHING
WWW.FULCRUMBOOKS.COM